WITHDRAWN

# The Wankel Rotary Engine: Introduction and Guide

# the WANKEL

Introduction and Guide

INDIANA UNIVERSITY PRESS

# ROTARY engine

HARRIS EDWARD DARK

BLOOMINGTON & LONDON

Published in Canada by Fitzhenry & Whiteside Limited,
Don Mills, Ontario

Manufactured in the United States of America


**Library of Congress Cataloging in Publication Data**

Dark, Harris Edward, 1922–
  The Wankel rotary engine.

  Bibliography: p. 129
  1. Wankel engine.   I. Title.
TL210.7.D37   1974   629.2′504   73-16676
ISBN 0-253-19021-5

To Phyl, who did the hard work, with love

# Contents

# Acknowledgments

For help in the compilation of the facts, figures, and events that make up this book, I want to thank Dr. Felix Wankel, the public relations and engineering departments of the Motor Vehicle Manufacturers Association of the U.S., General Motors Corporation, Ford Motor Company, Chrysler Corporation, American Motors Corporation, Curtiss-Wright Corporation, the Johnson Division and the Evinrude Division of Outboard Marine Corporation, Toyo Kogyo Company, Limited, and Mazda Motors of America, Incorporated.

Dr. Felix Wankel

# Preface

Felix Wankel did not invent the first, or the best, rotary internal-combustion engine. The rotary idea goes back at least to Agostino Ramelli, an Italian who in 1588 built a rotary water pump, and was furthered by James Watt, who proposed a rotary steam engine in 1759. John F. Cooley obtained patents in 1903 on an internal-combustion rotary, and the same type of engine was being worked on by the Swiss machine-tool company, Oerlikon, as early as 1911.

Wankel's rotary-engine designs have been vastly improved upon by Germany's NSU (now merged with Volkswagen's subsidiary, Auto Union), Japan's Toyo Kogyo (maker of the Mazda), America's Outboard Marine Corporation, and General Motors, among others. Undoubtedly, the best design is yet to come.

Wankel did, however, invent, and reinvent, the basic designs that most easily lent themselves to the development of the first *successful* rotary-combustion engine. And for that, the name of Wankel has already found its place in automotive history, where it will repose alongside the names of Otto, Duryea, Benz, Selden, Diesel, Ford, Olds, Kettering, and others later and perhaps greater.

In all automotive history there have been only two genuine engine revolutions: the nineteenth-century introduction of the internal-combustion engine to replace steam, and the introduction of Wankel's rotary engine to replace the piston-type gasoline engine. The latter replacement is only now beginning and may require most of the last generation of the twentieth century. The majority of us here today will be able to watch it happen.

There has been much talk about the rotary's being only an interim engine—that better ones will come along to replace it. In our technology *all* engines are interim engines, and the piston-type most of us still own has enjoyed an interim of dominance lasting close to a hundred years. The Wankel won't last that long, and neither will anything else in this society of increasingly compressed technology. But the Wankel will contribute its share toward helping to clean up our air, and it will receive its share of the limelight for many years to come.

The piston was an unfortunate idea from the start, but it was the only idea that would work. A century of sweat didn't improve it much for humanity and the world in which it burned its fuel. As it got larger and more powerful, in fact, it became a dangerous polluter of the atmosphere. And it had to be turned around—made less powerful, less efficient, more costly and difficult to operate—in order for us to be able to live with it at all.

The piston engine probably couldn't have been improved enough to live with us. It needed to be replaced.

And now for the first time, perhaps we have a replacement.

# The Wankel Rotary Engine: Introduction and Guide

# 1  A Century of Something Else

The automobile was not a single invention attributable to one person. For centuries mankind had dreamed of building a self-propelled vehicle with more stamina, longer endurance, and greater dependability than any

**1**

animal could provide. Men knew that it would have to be a mechanical device on wheels, but they were stymied by their inability to find a fuel that could be converted to motive power.

A successor to the stagecoach was needed, and in becoming that the earliest automobile became a more or less unsuccessful predecessor to the locomotive. Nicolas Joseph Cugnot, a French engineer, built what probably was the first self-propelled vehicle, in 1769. Thus the first vehicles that could be called automobiles were steam-powered, with external-combustion engines that generated heat in one place and sent it, in the form of steam, to yet another place to be converted to mechanical power.

The first such devices were heavy and bulky, unfitted for the few "good" roads used by stagecoaches. The wheels had to be made in the form of rollers to prevent the great weight of the vehicle from sinking into sand and mud. The furnaces put out quantities of smoke, and the engines emitted bursts of steam and were terribly noisy, causing horses and oxen to bolt at their approach. They had to be fueled constantly and were plagued with performance failures, even fatal explosions. The great majority of people wanted nothing to do with them.

When the first steam buses finally began to overcome some of their basic faults—and appeared, at least to the most optimistic, to be potential bidders for people-and-freight transportation—they were legislated against in England.

Stagecoach operators and early railroad investors saw the danger to their future prosperity in allowing free use of the nation's roads to steam buses, and they were successful in ramming through Parliament the infamous Red Flag Law of 1865. That law limited self-propelled, road-using (that is, steam bus) vehicles to three miles per hour and additionally required that such a vehicle be preceded on the road by a man carrying a red flag. While other nations proceeded with the auto's normal evolution, in England it was stifled for thirty years until restrictive laws were repealed in 1896. In that year, the first

American automobile track race was won at Narragansett Park, Rhode Island, by a Riker Electric at an average speed of 26.8 mph.

A small internal-combustion engine had been patented by a Belgian-born Frenchman, Etienne Lenoir (1822–1900) in 1860. Fueled by illuminating gas, the one-cylinder 1½ hp engine had a top rotating speed of 100 rpm (a modern V-8 cruises at over 3,000 rpm), and the car in which it was installed in 1863 took an hour and a half to go six miles.

The big jump came just one year later when Siegfried Marcus, a German-born Austrian (1831–1899), reworked Lenoir's design into a two-cycle engine (seen today in motorcycles, outboards, and some power mowers and snowmobiles) with a carburetor to handle liquid fuel and an electric-spark ignition. Many other experimenters became fascinated by the idea of a small self-propelled vehicle capable of carrying its own fuel supply for a driving range of several hours (the idea of several hundred miles would have been fantastically far-fetched—there were no roads to speak of, there were no rubber tires, shock absorbers, or decent springs, and even the hardy didn't consider the automobile in their long-distance travel plans). Steam cars were improved to a high degree of proficiency, but—especially in view of the Riker Electric victory—many people thought that electricity, the greatest servant of mankind, would provide the answer to automotive power.

Even as late as the beginning of this present century few would have bet that the internal-combustion piston engine—even though installed in many different brands of cars and already putt-putting around the streets of most of the world's major cities—would be likely to take over the industry in just a few more years to the virtual exclusion of all the other types. Today, many believe that the industry was wrong in allowing the takeover of the "gas buggy," their feeling being that the prodigious amount of time and design money squandered on the gasoline-piston would have produced more satisfactory

3

transportation if spent on one or more of the other types, particularly the two strongest contenders, the steam engine and the electric motor.

Between 1896 and 1917 the steam car was developed to a high degree of excellence, notably under the aegis of the Stanley brothers, who produced about 650 cars a year. But it was quite expensive, slow in start-up time, and burdened with the ever-present danger of explosion. Nevertheless it was powerful and fast, held the attention of the public for a number of years, and came closest to displacing the gasoline-piston. If most of the cars on the road today were powered by external-combustion steam engines, there probably would be no pollution problem, assuming that the steam engine had received the lavish investment in development devoted to the gasoline-piston.

Likewise the electric. Soon relegated to the category of a little-old-lady's car, the electric had the problem of not being able to carry along enough fuel to allow it to travel at what we now call freeway speeds for a long day's journey. The electric motor was perfected generations ago, and it could have eliminated transmissions, with all their problems, and differentials, with their losses of efficiency, by providing a motor for each wheel. To some extent, brakes and their energy losses also could have been displaced by using "engine retardation" to partially recharge the batteries used for fuel supply. But electrics were bypassed and suitable batteries were never invented. Electric forklift trucks were developed for warehouse use, and electric golf-carts became popular—slow-speed, un-spectacular-performance utility—but not for the highway.

If electrics had been more fully developed years ago, it's possible that most of our automotive power now being provided by a dwindling petroleum supply would instead be furnished by hydroelectric dams, a clean way of capturing energy from nature. As it is, much of our supply of electricity now comes from coal-burning power plants that are not so clean; and if today we should suddenly switch to electricity for automotive

4

power, the present production facilities for electricity would not be able to cope—they barely scrape by each summer when Americans turn on their air conditioners. But if things had *started out* differently—and, for example, we could be using that enormous supply of Montana coal or Colorado oil-shale for fuel in highly developed *clean* power generators that supply our electric needs—we might today be getting along just fine.

If, for example, we were getting our automotive power from coal burners carefully controlled by the utilities people, our cars would not be polluting downtown areas; they would be running on coal burned last night at some outlying utilities location. The burning would be controlled and highly efficient, not something done in each vehicle, in masses of vehicles of varying condition and pollution potential. We may never know whether sticking with the gas-piston was the tragic mistake it now appears to be.

What we do know is that early in the game, standards-to-stick-by became the *modus operandi* for the automotive industry. The piston looked so good for the first thirty or forty years of its life that no one but the most radical designers would consider switching to something else. Now in all fairness, certain things about the burgeoning industry should be considered. First, when an apparently successful improvement came along, everyone jumped into the act. This is understandable. A demand for autos began to outstrip supply, and everyone who wanted a job could go to work for any one of the *forty-two major* car manufacturers who were in business *before* the turn of the century. Before the great consolidations and cullings of the twenties, thirties, forties, and fifties culminated in what we now call the Big Four, more than two thousand makes of automobiles had been manufactured in the United States alone.

Even though America had begun its great love affair with the automobile in earnest by the early twenties, competition had become severe and great names were dropping by the wayside even before the Great Depression. The nation's most disastrous economic reversal wiped out more great names, and World War II finished off most of the rest. Finally even Packard, Studebaker, and Hudson joined the automotive limbo that was created primarily by economic conditions rather than the public's disfavor.

But from the beginning, the engineers-become-financiers were aware of the touchy economic tightrope they were walking (even Henry Ford came close to fiscal disaster at least once), and *changes* were things not to be taken lightly. Things could be added, things could be improved, things could be advertised as "new" or "exciting" or "the ultimate in automotive perfection"—but carefully.

There were incredible brake problems to be solved. And something had to be done about windshields to keep them from shattering, wipers to give the driver a chance to drive home in a sudden rainstorm, horns that were effective—and always tires, tires, tires.

In times like these, no sane designer felt disposed to bring up the possibility of a revolutionary change in the engines of his company's line of cars. For decades, Henry Ford refused to paint his cars a color other than black. It would be hard to imagine a directive from him authorizing research and development money for, say, a look into electrics (which were already successful in their own way), gas turbines (which were not new to engineers), or rotary engines (which were known before the name Wankel appeared on the scene), let alone the dozens of fresh ideas that must have occurred to inventors in the twenties, thirties, and forties.

You had a going thing, you didn't mess with it—that was the story in movie production, in advertising, in education, in everything, in fact, that was big and profitable and in severe competition. No underling was about to propose a revolutionary change to the boss of a large corporation that measured its profits and its share of the market in small percentage points. The piston engine fueled by gasoline worked, had worked for generations, and its place in the industry was more than secure—it was unique and unassailable.

So more and more money was spent on it, but not for a change unless that change could be proved in advance to be a low-cost improvement and a *minor* change that would not inspire misgivings in the minds of the buying public—this had already been shown to be faulty progress.

Ford used the four-cylinder Model T engine for more than a decade, amassing a vast fortune thereby. His next model, the A, was less than successful with the Crash of 1929 to contend with. And only his belated adoption of the V-8 in 1932—using pre-World War I ideas—restored and preserved his competitive position. It was a long time before his successors in his own company were willing to contemplate a six-cylinder engine, and even longer before the four-cylinder power plant—after being proved by competitors—was again put into production. And withal, the internal-combustion piston engine remained the only type even worthy of consideration in the eyes of Ford engineers, who, incidentally, are considered among the most innovative and progressive in the world automotive industry.

Actually, the piston engine had a lot going for it. Besides being first and receiving the lion's share of all further development, it was satisfactory to the early engineers—and readily accepted by the public—for several reasons. It could be made in an infinite number of sizes—the bore of the cylinders could be designed in any desired size, the rods could be short, medium, or long, and there could be one or two cylinders, or four, six, eight, twelve, or sixteen.

It could be any shape, with cylinders in-line (lined up one behind another from front to rear), formed in a V with an even number on each side, flat-opposed with cylinders lying on their sides, or even radial, as in aircraft, the cylinders lying about a circle with the crankshaft in the center. Thus an engine could be tall, long, and narrow, as in an old Buick in-line 8, or almost square, as in a V-6 or V-8.

7

The valves could be in the block, cast beside the cylinders, or in the cylinder head, operating in an upside-down position for better engine breathing and greater efficiency. The camshaft, which operates the valves, could be at the side toward the bottom of the engine, or it could be an overhead type close to the valves-in-head for extra efficiency and maximum power. An engine could even have dual overhead camshafts.

The piston engine could have one carburetor or several, or two built into one. From a set of pulley wheels at the front of the crankshaft, belts could be installed to drive the fan, water pump, alternator, power steering, and air conditioning. Some later models also have belt-driven air pumps to supply oxygen to the exhaust manifold for anti-pollution afterburning of the exhaust gases.

The crankshaft of the piston engine can be connected through a clutch to a manual transmission, or directly to an automatic transmission, or even more directly to the driving wheels via a trans-axle arrangement. The engine can be mounted almost anywhere, and in its long history it has moved from under the passenger seat to the front, to the rear, and in some late-model sports cars, back to the middle position.

Because it has been redesigned so many times, the piston engine offers an extremely flexible package to the car designer. Since it comes in all sizes and shapes, the designer has a free hand in the configuration of the car body into which it is fitted. The piston engine, after many generations of development, is mechanically suited to today's traffic conditions—it idles well, has excellent acceleration, and is capable of 70 mph speeds all day long, with only occasional stops for fuel and a check under the hood. Through ingenious balancing and damping and cushioning, the inherent vibrations of the many reciprocating motions of its parts have been controlled to a large degree. The inherent noise from the many back-and-forth actions inside the engine has also been quite well controlled by massive lubrication and sound treatment, such as rubber mountings and

8

fiberglass packs in the engine compartment and under the instrument panel.

Through modern miracles of metallurgy, most of the serious problems of wear in its many parts have been solved. The average American car, *if properly maintained* (which it almost never is), is capable of 125,000 miles or more without a major engine overhaul. The modern engine doesn't "use oil" in the old sense of the expression—that is, it can go 2,000 miles or more between changes without needing a make-up quart. (Many manufacturers use a higher figure, 4,000 miles and even more, for advertising purposes. But then they except "heavy duty" driving, which includes the housewife's and office worker's short-trip, slow-speed driving.) The fact that modern cars can travel thousands of miles without losing oil means something— it means that the manufacturers, in the 1960s, after a half-century of trying, finally succeeded in getting the internal engine parts to fit together and stay well fitted even after thousands of miles of wear.

References to wastefulness and efficiency, applied to the same type of engine, the internal-combustion piston, may seem incongruous. But in any discussion of this kind, even opposite factors can be seen as relative to each other. The term *efficiency*, when applied to an automobile engine, is a niggardly quality amounting to somewhere between 15 and 20 percent of the no-loss ideal.

In the general class of heat engines to which the internal-combustion piston engine belongs, the purpose is to extract stored energy from fuel by burning it and then immediately and internally converting the resulting heat to mechanical energy, which is used to propel the vehicle. The inefficiency problem results from the fact that only a small amount of the heat from the fuel can be so converted. The greatest amount of heat, instead of pushing pistons, escapes through the exhaust system and through the cooling system that is necessary to protect the engine from heat damage, and via radiation to the under-hood air from the engine itself.

9

Part of the problem stems from inability to burn the fuel correctly and completely; each fuel charge of air and gasoline from the carburetor has only a short, set time in which to burn, expand, and push the piston as it is supposed to do. This time is so short as to be measured in milliseconds when the engine is running fast. So the fuel charge is still burning uselessly when it is exhausted from the engine, and the wasted fuel is part of the cost of driving a car.

There are only two ways to keep an engine from burning itself up: blast its outside with a large supply of air, or circulate a liquid to the inside and then cool the liquid with a radiator. Both methods are successful, but they direct to the outside air a lot of heat you had to pay for but couldn't use for propulsion power in your engine. Unfortunately for your pocketbook, at least 80 percent of the gasoline you buy is used to heat the outside air.

This wastefulness is inherent in all internal-combustion engines, including the Wankel rotary. It will not be solved in the foreseeable future, and is not part of the argument rotary versus piston. But there is an interesting side-argument to be taken up later that seriously affects the ecology: What, in addition to heat, is contained in the exhaust products of the various types of engines? At this point it is more important to examine the piston engine to see why it has persisted—to now and at least for a few more years—as the dominant engine of the automotive industry.

Today we see much in print about "alternative" engines—alternatives to the piston, that is—and the next few years will see much, much more discussion, because some serious thinkers are of the opinion that we can no longer live on the same planet with the piston. This is the crux of the controversy at the moment, and the dispute will not be settled during the next few years, perhaps not definitely in this century.

But there is no question about the piston engine's position in the automotive world. It is number one and will remain so for many more years. The steam engine, the electric, the gas turbine—none of these has approached the piston. On no other engine has such wealth, attention, and even love been lavished. Only the piston has won the Indianapolis 500; only the piston has broken coast-to-coast records; only the piston has been in every garage in this or any other country.

And so we come to a strange point in the industrial history of the world: the engine that probably shouldn't have made it did, with almost everyone's help, with all the research and development money, without ever having a serious competitor. Now, for the first time in automotive history, there's a proved contender. For the first time, displacement is more than just an automotive engineer's term to express the size of an engine in cubic centimeters or cubic inches—displacement is something that could happen to the piston engine.

But the piston is not just going to go away. It will have to be driven away with all the relentlessness of competition that first placed it in its almost invulnerable position and kept it there for such a long time. And nearly all the forces of the mighty automotive industry, the nation's biggest employer, are still on its side and will remain so until its case is virtually hopeless.

No mogul would presently entertain the idea of retooling one engine plant, let alone a battery of them, just to present the public with something new. Hundreds of millions of dollars are involved in the intricate automated engine plants owned by the stockholders of the Big Four alone. No sane executive would say, "There's a new engine on the market now. It's doing well. It might be better than what we've got. Therefore let's scrap our present production setup and switch over to the new engine." That's not how things are done when just four companies make all the cars.

This country had as many as two thousand automobile manufacturers, off and on, during its early industrial history. Then, it would not have been unusual for dozens of them to switch over to, say, the Wankel engine—if there had been a Wankel at that time that could have been used in an auto. Unfortunately, by the time the Wankel showed up as a serious alternative to the piston, the latter was entrenched, four companies were entrenched, automotive engine development had ground to a standstill, and no new contender had much of a chance. The piston is still supreme.

So a small Japanese company is making some inroads; so the American companies know what a Wankel engine is, and are testing it; so the biggest manufacturer in the world is going to put a few Wankel rotaries on the market; so the American competitors are readying their production facilities or are making plans to buy Wankel rotaries, if they prove out, as a matter of maintaining competitive status in the eyes of their stockholders. What proof is there that something revolutionary is happening? There is none.

But don't put your betting money on the fat cats. They've been proved wrong before (Airflow, Nash, Edsel, Corvair), and the funny little engine that goes buzz instead of clickety-clack might just prove to be more than they bargained for. The rotary, thanks to Felix Wankel, some other Germans, some Americans, some Japanese, and the world at large, might force the biggest engine displacement of them all.

# 2 The Need for a Revolutionary Change

The automobile we are familiar with began to emerge more than a hundred years ago when European inventors Eugene Langen and Nikolaus August Otto formed a company to develop the internal-combustion engine.

## The Wankel Rotary Engine

Fueled by coal gas, a two-cycle Langen-Otto was displayed at the Paris Exposition of 1867, where it attracted world-wide attention. It was shown in improved form at the Philadelphia Centennial Exposition of 1876 and excited much interest among Americans. By this time Otto had a four-cycle engine of the type used by all American-built cars today.

In 1885 he successfully operated a model on liquid fuel. It wasn't long before engines similar to the Otto were being made in the United States for pumping, generation of electric power, and in lumbering and marine applications.

On September 21, 1893, the Duryea brothers put America's first successful gasoline engine motor vehicle (not yet called "automobile") in operation on the streets of Springfield, Massachusetts. In 1896, J. Frank Duryea produced his third car and then built thirteen more from the same plans. This was the first instance in the United States of more than one car being built from the same design.

In 1900, for the first time, a gasoline car defeated steam and electric cars in a free-for-all race at Washington Park race track in Chicago. The mass production of gasoline automobiles was assured by two events early in 1901, and these historic happenings determined more than any other factors that the gasoline engine would win out—in business—over its only competitors, the steam engine and the electric motor. On January 10 the oil well Spindletop came in as a colossal gusher near Beaumont, Texas, indicating the greatest oil field yet found, which immediately caused the price of petroleum crude to plummet to below five cents a barrel.

About two months later, Ransom Eli Olds, who had been experimenting with steam-powered vehicles for several years and who, in 1896, had driven his own one-cylinder, 6 hp gasoline car on the streets of Lansing, Michigan, lost his Detroit factory in a disastrous fire. The only thing saved from the holocaust was an experimental curved-dash roadster.

In the only course that would allow the Olds Motor Works to get back into business, the great inventor used his only model as a prototype-in-perfection and sent out orders for parts and subassemblies on a subcontract basis to many small shops around the Detroit area. Most of the shops consequently became automobile manufacturers, Detroit became the Motor City, and automobile production, in the full modern sense of the word, was under way using gasoline power plants. That same year Olds went on to build a record 425 curved-dash Oldsmobiles and became the first mass-producer of gasoline automobiles in the world. The French word *automobile* was then about five years old.

Also in 1901, but in New York City, an automobile storage and repair station set up a facility for direct service of gasoline to automobiles. The first "bulk tank" was placed outside the building for safety, and it was connected by a pipe to a self-measuring dispensing device in the basement so that cars could be serviced without handling and pouring of the dangerously flammable liquid. Nine years later, in 1910, Central Oil Company of Detroit opened what may have been the first drive-in gasoline station complete with an island and pumps for dispensing gas.

A year later a sixty-day guarantee on new automobiles was promulgated by the National Association of Automobile Manufacturers, which at that time had no less than 112 members. That same year a man in Minneapolis was arrested and fined ten dollars for "speeding" in excess of the maximum posted figure—10 mph. Oldsmobile production passed the two thousand mark for the year 1902, and the young Locomobile became the first American gasoline car with a four-cylinder, water-cooled, front-mounted engine.

In 1905 large gasoline cars dominated the Fifth National Automobile Show at New York City's Madison Square Garden. There were 177 gasoline cars on display, as opposed to only 4 steam cars and 31 electrics including 9 electric trucks. By 1906 six-cylinder cars were gaining in popularity. The following brand names offered sixes: National, Stevens-Duryea, Ford, Franklin, and Pierce-Arrow. By 1907 gasoline economy runs

15

were stylish, with one of the most popular being conducted in Chicago. In 1908 the first Model T Ford was offered.

At the Ninth National Automobile Show in 1909, four-cylinder cars had 71 percent of the displays and 27 percent were sixes. Only two one-cylinder models were offered. Louis Chevrolet, the famous race driver from Switzerland, started work on a six-cylinder passenger car in his Detroit shop and the White Company built a gasoline-engine car to replace the famous White Steamer.

By the end of 1909 there were 290 different makes of automobiles produced at 145 cities in 24 states. The city of Detroit had 25 car makes, of 45 produced in Michigan. Chicago had 14 different brands, Indianapolis had 12 and Cleveland had 10. After Michigan, Indiana was second with 44 brands and Ohio was third with 39.

In 1913 two important automotive advancements took place: the popularity of the Model T led to the use of a "body drop" for mass production, in which wholly completed bodies were lowered onto chassis constructions; and installment paper was used in automobile financing. In this year, apparently for the first time, there was evidence of concern on the part of automobile dealers regarding sales of used cars.

The next year, Cadillac introduced a high-speed V-8 engine, and the year following, 1915, eight-cylinder engines were the big talk at the National Automobile Show, featured not only in Cadillac cars but also in the King, Briggs-Detroiter, and Remington. By 1916 no less than eighteen models offered V-8 engines, including Abbott, Apperson, Briscoe, Cadillac, Cole, Daniels, Hollier, Jackson, King, Monarch, Oakland, Oldsmobile, Peerless, Pilot, Ross, Scripps-Booth, Standard, and Stearns-Knight. The first Chevrolet V-8 was offered in 1917.

Note that of this group, only Cadillac, Oldsmobile, and Chevrolet are still in production, under the aegis of General Motors. Of the others, only the Abbott, Apperson, and Peerless became well-known. The Abbott died in 1917, the Apperson in 1926, and the Peerless in 1932.

A few more facts will show the continued rapid development of the gasoline piston engine: In 1919 Ford produced 750,000 Model T's, more than one-third of the industry's total output. The following year Ford passed the five million mark in total production, by which time he alone had accounted for 55.45 percent of the American industry's total output.

On December 9, 1921, Dr. Thomas Midgley, Jr. and associates (including Charles Kettering) proved the effectiveness of a complicated and highly toxic chemical compound, tetraethyl lead, as an anti-knock additive in gasoline. On February 2, 1923, "Ethyl" gasoline was first sold, in Dayton, Ohio, by General Motors Research Corporation. The availability of Ethyl made possible a giant step forward in the development of the piston engine.

When air mixed with gasoline is taken into an engine in the form of a vapor it is compressed before it is ignited by the spark plug. The compression greatly enhances the fuel's ability to burn evenly and provide heat, which, in the form of a rapidly expanding gas, gives the push to the piston that is converted to power by the engine. Up to a point, the greater the compression the better the fuel burns.

A limiting factor, however, is that the compression itself causes heat, which if excessive will fire the fuel, usually at the wrong time, spoiling the critical spark-timing of the engine, and usually in the form of an explosion (detonation) instead of the even-burning function needed in a smooth-running engine. Addition of a small amount of tetraethyl lead, such as a teaspoonful per gallon of gasoline, tends to suppress detonation.

With the advent of the improved fuel, engineers were able to design greater and greater compression into their engines, making them more efficient and consequently more powerful without making them bigger. But because they were designing for an American market, the engineers also made the engines bigger, so cars would have a quicker acceleration rate, better passing ability on the highway, and a faster top speed.

17

## The Wankel Rotary Engine

It was Ethyl more than any other single invention that made possible the infamous horsepower race that followed World War II. The high-compression engine overdid itself, however, by producing an exhaust product heavy in the three main elements of present-day air pollution: unburned hydrocarbons, carbon monoxide, and nitrous oxides, the latter being NOx to the chemist and called "nox" for short. Nearly a decade after air pollution by automobiles became a big issue, the compression ratios of high-compression engines were reduced by as much as 20 percent. Some famous engines were reduced from a compression ratio of 10.5 to 1—to 8.5 to 1.

When an engine becomes worn it develops internal compression leaks. If the wear is even, so that the engine continues to run smoothly, the only noticeable malfunction is a loss of power and a consequent increase in fuel consumption. The forced reduction of compression ratio in late-model engines had the same effect, and now many brand-new engines have less power and lower gas mileage than engines of comparable size that are five to ten years older and half worn out.

That's only part of the bad news on late-model piston engines. The tendency during the years following World War II was to make power plants not only bigger and stronger but also more complicated and costly. For reasons to be discussed in greater detail in Chapter 7, the piston engine has an enormous number of precisely fitted parts compared to electric motors and other types of engines such as steam, gas turbine, and the Wankel rotary. To some extent the nature of the automobile business contributed to this—it is expensive to make changes, and severe competition dictated that costs be kept to a minimum. So sometimes, instead of completely redesigning a system when a change was necessary, a compromise would be made by merely adding a part here and there.

The simple engines of the twenties and thirties were mass-produced with only a few hundred parts, while today's power plants may have between one thousand and two thousand parts each. Moreover, new accessories were thought up, either to

18

improve the operation of the engine, to make driving easier and more comfortable and faster, or simply as sales tools to increase the share of the market. Often there was good and sufficient reason for an addition. For instance, shortly after automatic transmissions were introduced it was discovered that they should be cooled, like the engine, to prevent excessive wear and damage. So a pipe (with a necessary return pipe) was run forward past the engine to the radiator, through which transmission oil could be pumped, cooled in the radiator, and returned to the transmission. This had only a negligible effect on the operation of the engine.

On the other hand, the electrical systems of automobiles were gradually increased over the years until now they are more complicated than those found in the most modern homes. No one denies that backup lights, turn signals, and electric windshield wipers were fine ideas that contribute to safety. But whether it is necessary to hide headlights in the daytime or sit on a six-way seat is another question. Electric windows and seat, air conditioning, and a dozen other conveniences-become-necessities are a burden to the electrical system and call for a larger alternator and battery. And since all the "power" devices in a car receive their energy supply from the engine, it was inevitable that the mushrooming "power" demand would call for bigger and better engines.

The first automotive power was steam. The clumsy, heavy, dangerous steam engine was quickly overtaken in the market by the gas buggies and the electrics. Later, well into the twentieth century, the use of steam picked up again and some truly excellent steamers were put on the market. But they were large and expensive, and they suffered damage to their sales appeal through occasional but well-publicized explosions. Meanwhile, people were being burned in gasoline accidents, too; and they were being run over and crashed into by the cantankerous and ubiquitous gasoline-engine automobiles—but that was considered par for the course by a greater and greater percentage of the population, who were gradually coming to the idea that if you were somehow hurt by a car it was your own foolish fault. America was beginning its love affair with the automobile.

Under a 1.46 million dollar contract negotiated by the California legislature with Aerojet Liquid Rocket Co. of Sacramento and a 1.36 million dollar contract with Steam Power Systems, Inc. of San Diego, two experimental steam-powered subcompact cars already built have scored well on the low-emissions scale, it was reported in 1973 by *Automotive News*. Designed to operate in city traffic as well as on the freeways, the cars are capable of sustained speeds of 50 mph and can achieve as much as nineteen miles per gallon of gasoline on the highway.

When the project was started in 1972, gasoline consumption was not considered a priority compared with low engine emission and driveability. However, Roy Renner, technical manager of the program, reported that his team would, hopefully, improve fuel economy through transmission refinements and other modifications that can be achieved in time for the mid-1974 delivery date. These little cars undoubtedly will prove to be valuable stepping stones in the further badly needed development of steam for automotive power.

The electric, which could never go fast or far, was rapidly being relegated to the category of an extremely conservative driver's car. The reasons for the slow pace and the limited mileage of the electric are interesting and indeed are right now receiving a long close look by a number of engineers, with the likely result that in the next few years, and certainly before the century is out, we will again be driving some electric cars.

The Russians, anticipating the time when imposing a limit on the number of urban vehicles will become necessary for reasons of air pollution and traffic congestion, are interested in the development of electric cars for urban use while still allowing combustion engines on rural roads and in intercity traffic. Yuri Dolmatovsky, the Soviet engineer who is head of a laboratory at the Research Institute of Road Transport, Moscow, sees a strong probability for electric-vehicle use in cities while the internal-combustion engine will be further developed in his country for sports cars for long distances and leisure-time driving.

He added, in a 1973 statement carried by *Automotive News*, that there are important qualities in an electric car in addition to its pollution-free operation and quietness. For example, he said, the electric can be made more maneuverable than a combustion vehicle, the controls are much simpler, and its electrical brakes are more efficient, so that the driver is less likely to make a mistake.

Whether the electric motor is capable of displacing other types of power plants in cars is presently the subject of great controversy, however. The issue will not be resolved in the foreseeable future, not, in fact, until a sizable technical breakthrough has occurred. Here's why:

The scientist will tell you that all energy comes from the sun. We obtain it from a number of secondary sources. Energy from what we normally think of as fuel is usually the type that was stored by the sun during previous years or eons. Energy we obtain from burning wood, for example, was stored only during the growing life of the tree. But energy from fossil fuels such as petroleum and coal was invested by the sun during past eons when enormous forests were put in storage by cataclysms and the evolution of the earth's crust.

Wind, a vast and relatively untapped source of energy, is a function of solar power. The sun heats portions of our atmosphere, causing changes in the weight, or pressure, of the air that surrounds the earth. Inequalities in the temperature and pressure of the atmosphere are the chief causes of wind. There is now much interest in the possibility of the pollution-free generation of electricity via the installation of windmills in the mountains and plains, where the sun has stored energy in fairly dependable winds.

The sun also stores energy in water, but in a completely different way. The sun's rays pull water vapor up from the

**21**

oceans and mix it with the atmosphere. Later, that water condenses into droplets and rains down on the earth, or returns to the earth in the form of snow, often at altitudes higher than sea level. The rainwater and melted snow are constantly being pulled downwards across the land to the sea by the force of gravity. Man builds dams to store the water and, by directing it through turbines, makes the water generate electric power. Electricity, then, is heat from the sun converted to a form we can send over wires to where it is needed. It then is reconverted to heat, light, and mechanical power via resistance coils, filaments or gas bombardment, or motors, respectively.

When the sun stores the energy for us—in hydrocarbon or hydroelectric form—we have little trouble taking it out of storage. But when we try to store energy ourselves, we find it impossible to do so efficiently.

The modern driver thinks nothing of jumping into his car, accelerating to a high speed, and driving as much as two hundred miles or more before stopping for fuel, such is the tremendous amount of power stored by nature in a twenty-gallon tankful of gasoline. If a steam-powered car fired by either gasoline or oil were available, it could perform from the standpoint of speed and mileage at least as well as one with a gasoline engine.

But the electric car is something else. Electricity is not easy to store. The battery (actually a "battery" of chemical cells), in which electricity can be used to make sulfuric acid combine with plates of lead, is the only practical method of storage yet discovered.

But the problem is that only relatively small amounts of energy can be stored in batteries of reasonable size. In present-day technology, to jump into an electric car, accelerate to 70 mph and travel at that speed for two hundred miles would require that your car drag a trailer containing thousands of dollars worth of batteries.

Another, perhaps more serious problem, is the time needed to recharge electric-car batteries—and the facilities for doing so.

We're used to stopping for perhaps ten minutes for a "recharge" of our gas tank. Recharging two hundred miles worth of batteries under our present technology would take several hours, perhaps all night, so that daily mileage would be severely limited. Batteries could be exchanged, of course, in a few minutes, with the driver leaving his played-out set and taking on a newly charged supply. But that's a whole new industry that hasn't started up business yet.

The worst problem of all in electric-car technology, however, hasn't even been faced. The entire nation, now and for the foreseeable future, is distressingly if not dangerously short of electric power. We barely make it through the summer air conditioning months with frequent serious if not disastrous breakdowns in our grid systems. This will get worse before it gets better. The energy consumed by our automotive vehicles each day is many times the amount of energy used in the form of electricity for lights, motors, and home heating. If automobiles were suddenly to come out of the factories with motors instead of engines, the utilities companies would shortly blow all their fuses. That won't happen suddenly, of course. But many years before it begins to happen (and it almost certainly will happen), enormous increases in our electric supply will have to start building up to handle the added burden.

Such a revolution would immediately begin to clean up our air, incidentally. Every gasoline-piston engine taken out of service and replaced by an electric motor would move the burning of hydrocarbon fuel from our streets and inner cities to outlying areas and would put the necessary burning under strict quality control where it would do almost zero damage to the environment. Moreover, it would allow the use of vast untapped resources of coal and oil-shale to help preserve our dwindling supplies of petroleum and natural gas.

But best of all, it would switch much of our energy-garnering resources from the burning of gasoline and diesel oil to no burning whatsoever, if adequate hydroelectric facilities could be constructed in time to handle the load.

### The Wankel Rotary Engine

The simplest type of internal-combustion engine—yet one that has reached a high degree of development—is the gas turbine. Essentially a torch that blows on a fan, the gas turbine is most familiar in the turboprop and pure-jet engines used in aircraft, where problems of noise and fuel consumption are not so critical as in automotive traffic.

The first practical turbocar, the JET 1, was announced in 1950 by the Rover Company of England. Fiat of Italy had a turbine sports car in 1954, and a few years later Renault of France broke performance records with its turbine-powered *Étoile Filante*. Rover produced later versions of its car, and Leyland of England had trucks while another English car maker, Austin, produced both cars and trucks during the same period.

In the United States, Chrysler, General Motors, and Ford have all done extensive research in gas turbine engines. Ford and GM have concentrated largely on the development of turbines for commercial vehicles, and many responsible engineers expect turbine-powered buses and trucks to be a reality in the marketplace before 1980. Chrysler, on the other hand, did more experimenting with passenger-car applications than any other manufacturer. Beginning in the fall of 1963, Chrysler placed fifty turbocars on the road, in the hands of the public, on a loan basis. As the cars were passed from one "customer" to another, 203 people got to drive them about three months each, for a total of nearly 1,300,000 miles. The main purposes of the massive test were to determine the marketability of the innovative package and to wring out any inherent defects.

The engine had two main advantages: It was quiet (except for a whine at its high idle speed) and smooth, being entirely rotary in function with no reciprocating parts. It had several disadvantages, most of them minor and not insuperable:

> Could not provide air conditioning.
> Excessive gas generator rotor lag.
> Slow cold-starting.
> Inadequate engine braking.

24

Poor fuel economy in traffic.

Excessive weight.

Limited life of some components.

Although the engine was basically simple, with only one-fifth the number of parts found in a comparable piston engine—and was virtually maintenance-free—some of the parts were very high in manufacturing cost.

Many corrections have since been made in further research following this fourth-generation design. On a later engine many of the accessories such as air conditioner, alternator (alternating-current generator producing for a twelve-volt system), and power steering—originally driven unsatisfactorily from the gas generator shaft—were moved to the power turbine. This improved driving quality and decreased noise as many reduction gears were eliminated. With a new twelve-volt electrical system, fast and reliable starts became routine even at − 20 degrees F. Engine braking, by 1973, had been improved to equal or surpass that available from piston-engine retardation. Fuel economy was improved but is still slightly lower than that of a piston engine at low car speeds and idle. Continual modifications and accelerated endurance testing improved component life to the point of dependability at least up to 3,500 hours (100,000 miles of normal engine use), and by 1973 many parts had successfully accumulated 4,000 hours.

Yet any plans for production of the gas turbine were shelved by Chrysler for an entirely different reason: the provisions of the Clean Air Act of 1970. The gas turbine has tolerable unburned hydrocarbon and carbon monoxide emissions, but its NOx emissions are too far above the limits specified for the years 1975 and 1976 (for passenger cars) to make the engine feasible. Almost all of the disadvantages of the gas turbine, however, appear to be outweighed by the advantages in such an engine for big commercial vehicles. So while Chrysler has at least temporarily postponed production plans for its turbocar, Ford and GM will likely have production trucks and buses on the road in the next few years.

## The Wankel Rotary Engine

A broad analysis of future automotive engines was reported by the Eaton Corporation (mainly known as a famous axle manufacturer) in late 1973. The study, headed by R. W. Richardson, Eaton's manager of technological planning, dealt with engines "most likely to succeed" in the near future. One conclusion of the report: "On balance, the Stirling engine appears potentially the most attractive power plant over the long range."

The Stirling is an external-continuous-combustion engine that utilizes positive-displacement piston compression and expansion. Involved is a sealed high-pressure working fluid—for now, either helium or hydrogen. The engine operates at relatively low speeds.

Invented in 1816 as a pumping engine in mines during the nineteenth century, the original engine used compressed air as the working fluid. N. V. Philips of the Netherlands has researched and refined the Stirling in recent years and licensed both General Motors and Ford for development work. There are a few other licensees. GM accomplished much testing during the 1960s but let its license lapse in 1970. Ford was licensed in 1972 and at the end of 1973 was still working with Philips on passenger-car prototypes.

"The Stirling has a fuel consumption potential lower than any other contender and will operate on the broadest range of fuel," according to the Eaton study.

A number of auto manufacturers have experimented with the diesel engine, a high-compression internal-combustion piston power plant similar to the gasoline engine. The diesel can use a heavier fuel, an oil of the home-heating type, which has more British thermal units (BTUs) of energy per gallon than gasoline, and therefore provides more miles per gallon of fuel economy. Of great importance is the additional fact that the diesel has a somewhat cleaner exhaust than the gasoline engine.

The Mercedes of Germany, the Perkins of England, and the Peugeot of France are among the most prominent small diesel engines for automobiles. Diesels are more expensive and noisier than gasoline engines, and they do not have the typically fast acceleration motorists have come to expect from automobiles; but world-wide air-pollution problems and the increasing shortages and escalation of price of gasoline have greatly increased the interest in the diesel as an automobile power plant.

The time for a revolutionary change is long past. Just as it reaches its peak of dependability, the piston engine reveals itself as a poisoner of mankind. And just during the past few years mankind has decided that the piston engine stands before us condemned. It is being given one last chance to reform itself via a cease and desist order in the matter of air pollution, and it may be able to comply. But in doing so it will become much more expensive for us to own and operate, more difficult for us to use in the manner we've become accustomed to, and maybe—just maybe—we will find that our love affair was only a silly infatuation after all.

We may get tired of having to overfeed it day after day; we may decide that 15 to 20 percent efficiency is not good enough; we may find that adding more and more parts does not add up to better and better quality; we may discover that what we considered a smooth-running engine wasn't so smooth after all, and we may eagerly take up the cause of the first practical alternative ever offered us—the Wankel rotary.

True, it took several generations of living with the piston for us to learn that it may after all have been an unfortunate invention, that alternatives should have been more avidly encouraged years ago. But now that an alternative has been invented, tested, and tried, there's a good chance that the Wankel rotary and its upcoming successors-in-line will give the piston engine a really hard time in the market of the late seventies. The Wankel is all set to attempt just that, and it has some great things going for it in its appeal to Americans—almost zero pollution, quietness, vibration-free performance, small and light packaging under the hood, and others.

27

### The Wankel Rotary Engine

But of the others, one is outstanding, and you've been seeing it and hearing about it on television since it was determined to be hot advertising copy by its promoters in mid-1973—its fantastic acceleration rate as a power plant for the Mazda. Not the best recommendation for an engine from the social standpoint, but one that will appeal to many Americans, including most engineers, acceleration sells cars. Any experienced dragster will tell you that to have championship acceleration an engine must be nearly perfect. And the Mazda has it.

# 3 Harbingers of Inevitable Change

In 1950 more than eight million motor vehicles were sold in this country. This occurred in the middle of a period when vast numbers of Americans were moving to California for a number of good reasons—mild climate, a general rise in prosperity there due to increased industrialization and agricultural production, and the glamorization of the whole state by the motion picture business.

Soon there were more automobiles in California than in any other state (in fact, half again as many as in the second state, New York) and more than in the entire country of England. Although many cars were shipped and driven to California to take up residence there—and a virtual bumper-to-bumper tourist trade brought in additional millions on a year-around basis—many cars and trucks were being manufactured in California.

This created an industrial setup of steel mills, aluminum plants, tool and die shops, parts and accessory manufacturers, a huge dealer organization, and an enormous group of satellite retailers such as upholstery shops, wholesaler-retailer parts jobbers, garages and service stations the like of which exists nowhere else in the world. Soon California alone had more and better-quality roads than any other state or, for that matter, most foreign nations.

California also topped the nation's automotive picture with an asset claimed by few other states or nations: it had its own fully integrated fuel supply—wells, refineries, bulk stations, hauler fleets, service stations—and was in fact an exporter of gasoline. That asset is significant in its own peculiar air-pollution problem.

Drilling for oil is basically a clean business in that, except for accidents, any pollution can be kept confined to a small area. Whatever pollution results from spillage in land drilling usually flows harmlessly to the nearest low spot where it can be recovered from the land surface. The exception is off-shore drilling where, in case of accident, the oil gets away and can be reabsorbed only by nature.

In both off-shore and land drilling, fire is a constant hazard, and when a well-head fire occurs there is monstrous contribution to air pollution. In our present technology we generally must attribute such an occurrence to "unavoidable accident," and most sensible people are willing to accept that. But at the same time, the oil companies have put forward the story that—excepting the "unavoidable accident"—their operations are hound's-tooth clean. They will tell you that everything they operate is under absolute control. They can take you through a refinery that cost hundreds of millions and show you, for example, that the entire process of refining crude oil is automatic, operated by computers, and not subject to human miscalculation. They can show you that everything is sealed, that the crude goes in one end and comes out the other end in a variety of forms that benefit mankind without ever seeing the light of day. There is a maze of pipes, valves, control devices, and an abundance of what the petroleum engineer would call "technology."

Public relations people work hard to convince you that their company is doing everything it can to preserve the environment, and in what sometimes appears to be an excess of generosity (considering the severe competition involved) they will tell you that other major companies in the oil business are also doing their best.

But on the subject of air pollution there is one angle that more Americans ought to be interested in. You can go to an oil refinery and see all the fancy plumbing. You can listen to the public relations people trumpet the virtues of a "closed system" at the refinery that never lets anything get from the inside of the plumbing to the outside air. And then you can use the best detector there is—your nose. And if you do this, you'll become aware of a sickening, rotten smell (the natural odor of petroleum crude) that pervades the whole atmosphere of the place. Once aware of this, you'll notice it even as you go away (you'll also remember that you first noticed it when you were still some twenty miles from the refining area) and you'll have to admit that the odor of newly exposed ancient fossils brought up from the bowels of the earth permeates the air in the vicinity of an oil refinery.

Now Southern California catches air pollution from many

sources—oil refineries, motor vehicles, power generation by combustion, and others, not necessarily in that order of importance. Southern California is the worst possible place for air pollution and the Los Angeles Basin is the most unfortunate location in Southern California. Surrounded on three sides by hills of considerable altitude, the Los Angeles area suffers three-quarters of the time from a natural phenomenon called temperature inversion.

Normally, warm air rises in the heat of the day and cool air slides down the mountainside in the evening. The next day when the night's cool air is warmed by the sun it rises and is replaced that evening by more cool air from higher elevations. This generates a natural circulation that will frequently clean out the dirty air that envelops every population center. The insults of mankind even help the process along sometimes when, for example, industry, home heating (or air conditioning), or automotive traffic heats the air, causing it to rise during the day.

But in Los Angeles another phenomenon also occurs with distressing frequency, as it does less often in most other big cities of the world: a temperature inversion, in which a mass of hot air develops high over the city, trapping the slightly cooler air at the surface so that the cooler air will not rise thermodynamically. Only a few hours of this situation can put Los Angeles in an emergency situation with no change of air while the polluting contributors continue unabated. The problem gets worse when the lower layers of air, shielded by the dense pollution itself, cannot be heated by the sun and so rise normally.

Then to bring matters to the critical point, the sun's powerful rays in low-latitude cities such as Los Angeles cause toxic changes in the dirty air overhead that result in photochemical smog, a super-polluting of the atmosphere that wilts such plants as lettuce and spinach, kills flowers (formerly a great money crop in Southern California, now reduced to approximately one-third its original size by smog), and sometimes kills people, quickly and dramatically during smog alerts or slowly via respiratory disease such as emphysema.

Dirty air has always been a problem in big cities. Anyone fifty years old who came from the country to visit St. Louis, Pittsburgh, or Chicago as a child probably remembers the funny taste of "coal dust" in his mouth. Smoke abatement laws were enacted by Parliament to protect London hundreds of years ago. But bear in mind that Los Angeles has had a most phenomenal growth, doubling in population from 1920 to 1930 and then almost doing it again in the next twenty years so that it had a population of nearly two million by 1950. This is the city only, not the county, which had a population exceeding four million by 1950 in no less than forty-five incorporated cities. Such concentration and resulting congestion runs against all reason in a relatively small industrial area jam-packed with autos and trucks and new factories and oil refineries.

But who is to advertise, "Don't come to Southern California —we're too crowded already"? Not any chamber of commerce in the business of promoting more and more industry. Not any local government looking for a higher and higher tax base. And not the average citizen with no advertising money to spend on his environment. So the Los Angeles Basin filled up—with people and with the results of their combustion. By 1960 the city and its widespread environs had experienced devastating smogs—to no one's surprise.

Future historians may say that it was "to the everlasting credit of the people of Los Angeles that they were first in the United States to battle successfully against automotive air pollution." The fact is that their backs were to the wall—it was fight or die. But give them this: the governments of Los Angeles and the State of California stayed one or two years ahead of any national efforts to combat air pollution, and indeed the state generally set the pattern for the laws that hopefully will restore clean air to the United States.

Dr. A. J. Haagen-Smit, a biochemistry researcher at the

### The Wankel Rotary Engine

California Institute of Technology, proved in 1951 that motor vehicles contribute to air pollution. He exposed samples of exhaust products to natural sunlight under carefully controlled laboratory conditions and showed that the resulting chemical changes produced gases that irritated eyes, aged rubber, damaged vegetation, corroded metal, and did all the other bad things that had been attributed to photochemical smog.

In 1959 (note: eight years later) the automotive industry announced that it was going to do something about blowby gases from the crankcases of its cars. Blowby is a form of exhaust product that, through a defect in the engine, finds itself in the crankcase instead of the exhaust pipe. It is a gas, consisting largely of air and unburned hydrocarbons, that is rammed past the rings of a piston engine due to leakage between the rings and the cylinder walls. This occurs to a slight degree in a new engine, but it gets worse as the engine wears.

Blowby is a small contributor of pollution compared to the exhaust products coming out of the tailpipes of hundreds of millions of American vehicles, but no matter—the auto makers jumped on it as a quick, easy, and, of utmost importance, *cheap* method of getting on the side of the angels.

Blowby has always been a technical problem with all conventional engines. The piston must fit inside the cylinder tightly so that it can provide compression to the combustion chamber and also be able to handle the enormous push of the expanding gases following ignition of the fuel. It is fitted with rings that are held by spring tension between it and the cylinder walls, and on its upstroke it receives a spray of crankcase oil to help seal the rings against the cylinder walls. In a new engine this method works almost perfectly, but from the beginning automotive engineers have been aware that engine wear begins here, and in order to achieve the 100,000-mile (or more) life that has become a standard in the automotive industry, steps were taken many years ago to manage the blowby that developed in worn engines.

An effective method had to be employed to get rid of the

gases that blew by the piston rings and tended to fill up the crankcase with unattractive vapors that loaded the crankcase oil with sludge. It didn't take much imagination. Somebody simply said, "Let's ventilate the crankcase." And it was done.

So in engines that pre-dated World War II there was a method for this important function. Cheap and simple, it consisted of an air intake to the crankcase and a pipe, usually on the opposite side of the crankcase, through which vapor-laden air could be exhausted. This, incidentally, had nothing to do with the exhaust system of the vehicle. The so-called road draft tube that carried away the extraneous exhaust products from the crankcase contributed greatly to engine life.

In this method the whirling motion of the crankshaft acted as a blower, sucking in air through the oil filler pipe and pumping air mixed with crankcase (blowby) vapors out the road draft tube. But somebody discovered that what went out the road draft tube contained unburned hydrocarbons similar to those in the exhaust gases, and the first anti-air-pollution system on automobiles became known as "positive crankcase ventilation."

PCV, as it is now called, is simply a method of utilizing a small portion of the intake manifold vacuum (the same vacuum that draws in the air-fuel mixture from the carburetor) to suck unwanted vapors from the crankcase and dump them into the engine to be burned along with the fuel. To do this the old ventilated cap on the oil-filler pipe was replaced with a non-ventilated one so that the pipe was sealed, and another pipe or hose was run to the air filter housing for a supply of clean air that could be pulled into the crankcase. Then on the other side of the crankcase a suction hose was installed to run to the intake manifold. Thus air was pulled from the air filter housing down into the crankcase, across the crankcase, and via the second hose to the intake system of the engine. In the second hose a valve was installed to limit the amount of suction that could be applied to the crankcase to avoid the possibility of sucking rich *oil* vapors from the crankcase and burning them, too. The PCV valve, then, became the first weapon in the fight against air pollution.

In what turned out to be another example of adding on parts to improve an existing design, however, the engineers left a flaw. The PCV valve, like the filters, belts, vacuum and water hoses, spark plugs, ignition points, etc., must be replaced with regularity. The hoses associated with PCV also need replacement from time to time like all other rubber parts under the hood. So the PCV valve, at about three dollars plus labor, joined the growing after-market sales business of the automotive industry more than ten years ago and by itself has accounted for many millions of dollars worth of new income for manufacturers, jobbers, retailers, and mechanics.

The PCV valve doesn't wear out but instead eventually becomes jammed with sludge. Once this happens, the now-sealed crankcase loses all its ventilation and accumulates sludge at a rapid rate. Uncorrected, this situation can "total out" an engine in short order, so replacement of the PCV valve is a must on a regular basis.

It has been noted that an older engine, if wear throughout it has been even and not severe to a point that could be defined as "damage," can continue to function almost as satisfactorily as a new one. There will be a bit more noise but it will be well enough absorbed by rubber engine mounts, fiberglass pads under the hood, and internal engine lubrication. Oil consumption will increase to the point where a makeup quart or two has to be added every thousand miles or so, and gasoline mileage will fall (often imperceptibly) because of the leaking by the piston rings of gases that are supposed to power the engine. But withal, an engine with 50,000 to 100,000 miles on it can be kept tuned and in fairly good running order.

However, an engine built during the past decade has a PCV system, and there is a limit to the amount of blowby gases it can handle. Although the engine may be functioning satisfactorily otherwise, blowby can become too much for the PCV system, pressure can build up in the crankcase, and then the engine will start to "throw" oil—up through the hose-pipe arrangement leading from the oil filler tube and directly to the air filter housing. This causes the air filter to jam and fills the exhaust system with unburned hydrocarbons from the over-rich carburetor mixture that results. It also feeds crankcase oil to the combustion chambers, causing additional pollution. Any minor attempt to relieve the excessive pressure would frustrate the anti-pollution function of the PCV system. But given the choice of a three hundred dollar "ring job" to correct the problem or a four dollar pipe to sidestep it, many auto owners can be expected to opt for the latter and go their merry polluting way.

That was the first problem to result from anti-pollution measures applied to the existing piston engine in an attempt to clean it up. The problem is now more than ten years old and can only get worse as old engines get older.

Even though the PCV system helped to prevent the dumping of some unburned hydrocarbons, by far the majority of pollutants continued to escape the engine via the exhaust system. In 1968 models a few minor attempts were made under increasing government pressure toward cleaning up exhaust products. These were mostly in the area of spark control, preheating of intake air, and in a few cases an innovative supplying of fresh air to the exhaust manifold, the object of all being to cause a more thorough burning of that portion of the fuel mixture that was being wasted due to incomplete combustion. With these changes, the first substantial modifications of old-time ignition and carburetion theories, engines began to get finicky. The basic engines had not been changed; adjustments were made *outside* the engines to make what went on inside them more palatable.

When motorists began to complain that their brand-new cars were hard to start, reluctant to warm up, difficult to keep idling correctly in traffic, subject to "after-run," and just plain cantankerous in general, the manufacturers, through their dealers, had a prepared answer: "By driving our new model you

**37**

are doing your bit for air conservation. The new cars are more critically adjusted to do a better, cleaner job of burning fuel. It's up to you now, as a motorist who wants to help clean up the air, to bring your car in more often for a tuneup." Again, more service business for the dealer and more parts for the manufacturer to sell to his captive market. Why "captive"? Because it would be a violation of warranty terms to install a non-"factory" part or have work done by mechanics employed by other than an authorized dealer.

Yet withal, the 1968, 1969, and 1970 models were paragons of smooth-running virtue compared to those that followed. For beginning with the 1971 models, really drastic revisions of the old principles of engine design had to be instituted under federal government order. Chief among these was reduction of compression ratio. As mentioned previously, engine design had progressed into the 1960s with higher and higher compression ratios to provide better combustion efficiency, which meant more power for acceleration and better fuel economy.

But this was the age of the "muscle car," and engines were also being built bigger and bigger. Soon cars had so much power that a driver could "lay rubber" for a city block after starting from a standstill. It should also be mentioned that immense advances had been made in metallurgy and gear technology, so the drive train—from the engine's crankshaft to the wheels—was able to stand the strain. The broken axle, once a plague to the driver, became almost a thing of the historic past.

The designers of large cars—Cadillac, Imperial, Continental— had to lead the horsepower race to keep their products away from the image of slow, lumbering "battleships" with no get-up-and-go. With the resources they had at hand they were able to do this with remarkable success.

Cadillac, for example, enlarged its already monumental engine from 429 cubic inches (at least 100 cubic inches larger than the medium-size engine found in "standard"-size cars) to a whopping 472 cubic inches in its regular 1968 models, and to

500 cubic inches in the Eldorado. Now the luxury cars used more gasoline but that didn't surprise anybody; if tested on a ton-mile-per-gallon basis—which takes into consideration the extra weight of the big car—their fuel consumption was quite acceptable.

When in the 1971 models certain drastic changes had to be made to comply with stringent government regulations regarding exhaust product, however, automotive engine performance in matters of power dropped back almost twenty years. But that wasn't the worst of it. The really bad news was that these great engines with their century of development had not only been emasculated in power but also had had numerous obstacles thrown in their way in what the public had come to know as "performance."

Now the new engines were really hard to start if it was a bit chilly or a bit warmish; they had to be warmed up slowly before being pulled out of the driveway to prevent them from bucking and stalling in traffic; they were subject to after-run or "dieseling" more than ever before; tuneups on them were difficult, expensive, and often not satisfactory; they tended to backfire through the carburetor and caught fire a lot. In short, they were, and still are, a real mess, and the public is disgusted with them. The greatest injury to the American driver, of course, was the cutting down of his beloved power, causing him to have to be extra careful about allowing adequate passing distances. The loss of startup acceleration, though less dramatic, was an added injury to his pride.

But then the motorist learned that an unforgivable insult had been added: his new car was using a great deal more gasoline, sometimes twice as much as the older cars he had learned to love. Again, the manufacturers and dealers came forward with their solution: "Be a good American and help preserve our air by bringing your car in for more frequent tuneups."

# 4 Enter the Wankel Rotary

If the latter-day troubles of the piston engine—culminating in a degradation of power, a troublesome skittishness in performance, and a loss of fuel economy—were not almost more than the American motorist could be expected

40

to bear, another blow, perhaps the worst of all, struck him in 1973. For the first time since World War II, he had to face up to a gasoline shortage.

Although the shortage had had a buildup of several years, the reality of it—when the first few motorists pulled into their service stations in various parts of the country and were confronted with "out of gas" signs—hit with stunning force. It was big news immediately, and the media gave it enormous exposure, in many cases blowing it up out of all proportion. The easy thing to do, in performing this kind of coverage, is to find four or five service stations that are temporarily short or out of gas and then interview the owners of the stations. This only too often provokes a disgruntled station operator into expressing an exaggerated opinion, or it may cause an isolated situation to appear to have national significance. Worse, a network may pick out isolated shortages in, say, Philadelphia, Kansas City, Denver, and San Francisco and give the impression that gas pumps are going dry all across the nation.

Whichever way it happened, by April of 1973 it brought the American public to the edge of panic. People dared not plan long-distance vacation trips in the family car for fear they would get far from home and be stranded. The upshot was that there was some modification of vacation plans and some gasoline was conserved; but generally speaking the only inconvenience to the public was an isolated instance in which a customer had to make two or three stops for gas instead of his usual single stop for a tankful. In fact, in many areas gas wars continued throughout the summer and the transcontinental traveler found bargains everywhere.

After waiting in the wings for a modest period of time, the federal government entered the picture to "help out" panic-stricken consumers of gasoline. When the government officials applied their theoretical expertise to a simple practical situation of supply and demand, the usual result affronted the public: the government applied price controls to the retailers of gasoline without applying controls to the wholesalers, thus getting the ordinary filling station operator in an untenable bind. Enraged at the discrimination, gasoline retailers banded together and called local "strikes"—limited closings down—in a rash of protest movements from one end of the country to the other.

These actions were given even more attention by the media, personnel of which were fascinated by the idea of a "strike" by people other than members of organized labor unions. When, day after day, the public found itself confronted with "shut-downs" of gasoline service that often covered most of the outlets in areas as big as metropolitan St. Louis, panic grew and grew.

It now appears that what seemed to be a nationwide shortage was nothing more than a shortening in the gross amounts in bulk stocks here and there around the country. Typically, the major companies overproduce for the domestic market. This has been going on for several decades and has in fact sired the independent or "no-name" gasoline industry, consisting of wholesalers who buy at the wellhead, truckers, jobbers with their own bulk stations, and thousands of independent retailers who generally own their own stations rather than leasing or partially owning them, as is often the case with the major-brand business.

The independent suppliers obtain much of their gasoline from overrun stocks of the majors. A few of the independents got so big that they built refineries for crude oil they bought at the wellhead, and in some cases they actually owned some of the wells. But the biggest portion of their supplies had to be obtained from the majors. In 1973 the stocks of the majors began to shrink, and the majors became increasingly reluctant about keeping the independents, who after all are competitors, supplied. This put the independents in a tight spot and forced many small operators out of business.

No one yet knows what caused the majors' overrun stocks to dwindle. Many of the independents bitterly said it was a plot to trample the little guys. The majors cited a number of plausible reasons. Congressional investigation of the whole matter is probably the only sure way of getting all the facts, and that is in the offing.

But certain facts are obvious. The oil industry is continually threatened with loss of the depletion allowance, a tax exemption that has been as high as 27.5 percent of income to encourage exploration and expensive, risky drilling for new supplies. This threat tends to discourage development of new supplies. The Alaska Pipeline issue was precariously balanced in 1973, and the major oil companies wanted to make sure a favorable law was passed; threats of shortages turned out to be a powerful form of argument. The majors *may* have been trying to squeeze out at least some of the independents, to "clean up" the market in their own eyes. Many other factors, large and small, could have been involved.

The whole turmoil, picking up plenty of momentum by spring of 1973, had a strong influence on the economy. While traveling salesmen continued their motoring with little more than an occasional nuisance search for gasoline, vacation travelers gave their plans a hard look and frequently changed them in favor of shorter trips. People planning to buy large gas-guzzling automobiles often had second thoughts, either postponing the purchase or spending some time in small-car showrooms. Sales of motor homes fell off disastrously, in a few cases putting some of the industry's manufacturers in financial jeopardy.

Eventually many people who had never before considered the purchase of a small car got serious about trading the old family bus in for a little, sleek package that had suddenly become the "in thing" among their more conventional or conservative set. By midsummer, sales of small cars had leaped almost out of bounds, capturing some 40 percent of the new-car market, a share unprecedented in American automotive history.

The rush toward little-car buying was upsetting to the domestic manufacturers, which were selling more units but at much lower unit price tags. It was an incentive, however, for them to enlarge their small-car production facilities, which they hastily did. The same trend was a boon to the manufacturers of imports, most of which are small and sippers rather than gulpers of gasoline. Volkswagen, which had suffered several successive annual sales drops, perked up again, and in spite of a bad slide in the dollar (which increased the comparative value of the Deutsche Mark and effectively raised the cost of the VW to American buyers) began to reassume its high position among the imports. Other imports, from Germany, Italy, England, and France, were likewise enjoying new prosperity on the American market.

The Big Two among the Japanese imports, Toyota and Datsun, were riding the high road for two reasons: their low initial cost and their excellent fuel economy, both due to their small size. But a third Japanese automobile, the Mazda, a product of Toyo Kogyo, Hiroshima, had begun to make remarkable gains even before there was much talk of a fuel shortage.

The Mazda had something offered by no other manufacturer: a small, inexpensive *rotary*-combustion engine originally designed by the great German inventor, Felix Wankel. The Mazda name was also on a small but excellent four-cylinder, front-mounted, rear-drive engine, and these sold quite respectably. The Mazda was quickly recognized as a good little car. Its riding qualities are excellent, its brakes among the best, its body sound. The company offered a wide list of luxury accessories, including air conditioning, that took the Mazda out of the "cheap car" class in American eyes. Dealerships were assigned slowly at first, and although the car had been available for more than two years it was late 1972 before most Americans could visit a showroom without having to drive several hundred miles.

Nevertheless, the Mazda had received a remarkably good press among car-buff magazines, and several nationally known newspapers had carried articles that were favorable. So,

**44**

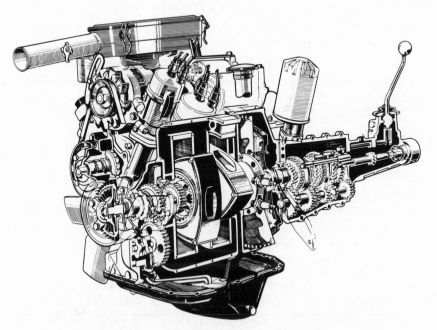

Cutaway drawing of the Mazda Wankel-type engine. The two spark plugs (shown "floating" here) are for the rear rotor; two plugs are also provided for the front rotor, to insure good ignition and more complete combustion.

without much corporate advertising, the dealers were selling just about all the Mazdas they could get their hands on. After the Mazda dealership system had been extended, by mid-1973, to cover every major city and a large number of others as small as the 100,000-population class, Mazda Motors of America, the U.S. sales arm, decided to phase out the four-cylinder engine (which, though excellent, was after all quite similar to those in a large number of competitors' cars) and concentrate its sales efforts on the Wankel rotary power plant.

By this time, General Motors had given every indication that the world's largest manufacturer would soon "join the rotary club," as many automotive writers and newspaper headline composers had chosen to phrase the idea. Everyone in the automotive journalism business seemed to agree that GM would indeed produce rotary engines, but no responsible reporter—and certainly no one really in the know at GM—was willing to say just when this might happen. Speculation ran rampant. In 1972 and 1973 GM had shown models or mockups of its rotary engine, but all the while top engineering and administrative executives had played it extremely cool, attempting to give the impression that GM was only mildly interested in the new type of engine.

Meantime, Mazda was selling them as fast—literally—as it could make them, and the formerly small Japanese manufacturer was expanding with every flexing of its wiry industrial muscles. The Toyo Kogyo people knew something that no one else knew for sure: they knew they had a hot commodity on their hands—a small car with a small engine for fuel economy, yes, but much, much more than that—an absolutely new engine, the like of which few people in the world had ever seen before, and just at the time when "changes" were the talk of the automotive industry. They also had something more, something of infinitely greater value from an emotional, advertising, and, therefore, sales standpoint: a *revolutionary* engine, the product of the very first technical revolution in the century-old history of the automotive industry.

46

Automatic transmissions, important stride forward that they were, were nothing more than the application of more mechanical principles and gadgets to the shifting of gears; shatterproof glass was merely an improvement in windshield design; four-wheel hydraulic brakes were simply an extension of what had gone before with an added improvement; electric windshield wipers were basically a switch from vacuum to electricity for more dependability. But even though engines had taken various sizes, shapes, and placement of cylinders, they were still *piston* engines with all their old faults and virtues.

Now, however, here was an engine that didn't fall into any of the previous categories—V, in-line, flat-opposed, radial—because it used the principle of internal combustion without having pistons or cylinders. Nothing like it had ever appeared before on the American automotive scene and been taken seriously.

But the Mazda rotary was here, on the road by the thousands, apparently a success. Now "success" is a word not to be taken lightly. In an engine it means, first and foremost, the ability to propel a car for more than 100,000 miles without the necessity of a complete teardown for overhaul. This was quite an order, a challenge to the piston engine, which already had a century of development and literally hundreds of millions of dollars behind it. Could the Mazda rotary stand the abuse— could it, with only a few years of development time, show its ability to stand up under American road conditions for 100,000 miles or more? No one knew for sure.

Automotive engineers have repeatedly said that it was one thing to build an engine and run it on a test stand; that it was another thing to put it into a car and travel it around a test track for thousands of miles; and that it was a third and completely different thing then to turn over that engine to the public, that as soon as old John Q. got hold of it he would find out the *real* things that were wrong with it.

Mazda engineers went through the test-stand routine over and over; they put cars on the test track for thousands of hours; but only the public, they knew, could give the Mazda rotary the final wringing out that would eventually spell success or failure for their engine.

The first "big" year of Mazda rotary production (1969) saw about thirty thousand engines come out of the factory. This was an impressive number representing more than $30 million (wholesale) worth of under-hood hardware. But for a fair comparison it should be noted that the total of thirty thousand engines was about equal to one and one-half days of production for General Motors.

Call it luck or call it good engineering—Mazda had very little trouble with its early production engines and felt confident about going ahead with full-scale manufacture. As you read this book hundreds of thousands of the little buzzers are zipping about the countryside without having any trouble. Talk to a service manager at a Mazda dealership, as a matter of fact, and he will tell you that most of the troubles he sees are those that result from "customer ineptness," polite diction for stupidity. (Problems that can develop in the Mazda rotary, how to prevent them, and what to do about them, are detailed in Chapter 9.)

It wasn't always so, this ability of the rotary engine to go a long distance without having any trouble. But for the stubbornness of Felix Wankel (a characteristic of most great inventors) and the dogged persistence of his Japanese successors, it is not likely there would be anything like the great number of successful Mazdas on the road today. The earliest rotaries, Wankel's as well as others, simply did not perform in the way the public had come to expect an automobile engine to perform. They were smoky (always a sign of serious trouble internally) and they didn't last long. But they *were* smooth, simply because they were rotaries, and that's what fascinated the engineers.

It is important to bear in mind that the first, second, and even the *one-thousandth* piston engine did not work flawlessly.

48

It could be said that the best piston engine on the market today is remarkably defective considering the millions of man-hours and the billions of dollars already invested in the development of it and its predecessors. In view of this, it is almost a miracle that the Mazda Wankel rotary was made road-ready in the few years it was under development by Toyo Kogyo at a cost of only $36 million. Add to this the fact that not much of the highly developed piston-engine information could be utilized in the Wankel rotary. The most important contributors to the success of the Mazda Wankel were computerized machining and space-age metallurgy—along with great quantities of dogged determination.

Felix Wankel was only one of a large number of top engineers and inventors interested in the idea of a rotary engine. The elimination of all reciprocating actions within the engine was the ideal most inventors aspired to, while others attempted to compromise here and there. It is now clearly evident that those who stuck to the pure-rotary principle—all parts moving in the same direction—were the most nearly correct in their thinking.

Wankel started his rotary engine work in the 1920s and continued it off and on for five decades. During that time many rotaries were attempted by others, and some became actual working engines. To mention a few:

The Eugene Kauertz (German) engine has vane-type rotors, resembling a pie with wedge-shaped pieces cut out of it, that revolve in a circular chamber. Although the two pairs of vanes spin on the same axis, they are not tied together and in fact continuously change position in relation to each other. One set of vanes at first slows down and then speeds up, providing compression of the air-gasoline mixture from the carburetor. When ignition occurs, the space between the vanes on the power stroke opens up as combustion pressure drives one vane away from the other. The other two vanes are meanwhile closing together to provide compression for the newest fuel

**49**

charge. The timing of the vanes is controlled by an external gearbox. Valving is done by the vanes, which open and close ports as they revolve.

The Traugott Tschudi (Swiss) engine has four curved pistons that revolve inside a closed track called a toroid. The pistons are carried in pairs on two rotors that ride on rollers bearing on cams, which are connected to the crankshaft. Compression between the pistons occurs like that between the vanes of the Kauertz engine as the pistons are alternately stopped and started by the cam-roller action.

The Virmel (American) engine, designed by Melvin Rolfsmeyer and named for his wife, Virginia, and himself, has two sets of vane-type pistons but with a gear-and-crank system to control the action.

The largest number of successful rotary engines so far, however, have been designed without the scissors sort of action associated with vanes and pistons. Instead, an eccentric rotor shaped like a slightly inflated triangle is geared to move inside a housing having the outline of a fat-figure-eight, called an epitrochoid. The Wankel is one of several of this type and it has been manufactured by NSU Motorenwerke AG, Germany, in association with Felix Wankel himself, and by several other engine makers including Curtiss-Wright of the United States, Sachs Motor Corporation, Ltd. of Canada, Outboard Marine Corporation of the United States, General Motors, and of course, by Toyo Kogyo of Japan, the builders of the Mazda, the first Wankel-powered automobile to be mass-produced.

Speculation on the road-readiness of the Mazda rotary engine at the time it was first offered for sale in the United States in 1970—which speculation continued for three years thereafter—has now ceased. In that first year only 649 rotary engines were put on the road, not a dependable sample for statistical purposes. In 1971, however, 11,623 were sold, and the figure jumped to 42,609 for the year 1972 and more than 119,000 for 1973 in the United States alone. By the beginning of 1974 Toyo Kogyo had a world-wide total sales of more than

700,000 rotary-engine automobiles. That figure is expected to continue to mushroom with the opening in late 1973 of a new engine plant that doubled the company's production capacity and the offering, early in 1974, of a pickup truck that is equipped with a rotary.

By 1974 many Mazda rotaries in the hands of the public have achieved an accumulated mileage of 80,000, and a few have gone well over the 100,000 mark without need for major overhaul. Thus Mazda is able to offer valid proof to the public that the Wankel rotary can be as dependable as the conventional piston engine—an aggregate of many millions of miles of genuine dependability. To the surprise of many people, the new and revolutionary engine actually develops *fewer* troubles than conventional piston engines. Perhaps this can be explained by citing the comparative simplicity of the rotary and its fewer parts, the vibration-free movement of those parts, and the rotary action in general, which seems to be less sensitive to abuse, especially the abuse of overrunning—"winding up" the engine in the lower gears—which spells quick death to a piston design.

The three supposed "weak spots" in the Mazda rotary—excessive wear to apex seals and rotor side-seals, plus premature failure of the plastic O-ring gaskets—have not turned out to be weak spots after all. Engines have been torn down after 50,000 miles to show such minimal wear to the seals as to project a normal life of 150,000 miles, and at 50,000 miles no abnormality showed up in the O-rings.

Opinions of future competitors to the contrary, of course, it appears that none of the gloomy forecasts have been justified. General Motors, which has its rotary in production for the first time in 1974, originally claimed that the materials and some of the designs in the Mazda were just simply not good enough to be used in a GM engine. Chrysler officials spent most of 1972 and 1973 talking down the whole idea of a rotary, and Ford threw it no bouquets. There is every indication in 1974, however, that such attitudes were little more than competitive

**51**

Interior view of one section of the Mazda Wankel rotary engine, showing positioning of the rotor within the epitrochoidal chamber. Note the tub-shaped depression on the rotor that forms part of the combustion chamber.

corporate propaganda, and it will surprise no one if talk begins slowly to swing around to the other side of the argument.

The fact of a GM rotary must now be faced, and it is inconceivable that large manufacturers like Ford and Chrysler will ignore what GM is doing.

Meantime, more and more Mazda Wankels hit the road every month, and three-quarters of a million successful engines can't be ignored either.

# 5   Felix's Bad Boy

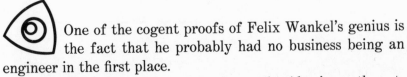 One of the cogent proofs of Felix Wankel's genius is the fact that he probably had no business being an engineer in the first place.

He was born in the Black Forest near the Alps in southwestern Germany on August 13, 1902, in the region called Swabia. Here people were farmers, lumbermen, wine growers, or craftsmen. His father, Rudolf, was a forest commissioner who was killed early in World War I when Felix was twelve years of age. At the time the boy graduated from high school at nineteen, postwar inflation had hit his country hard and Felix had to go to work in Heidelberg as a salesman for a publisher of technical books. Always interested in machinery, Felix managed to open his own workshop in Heidelberg at the age of twenty-two. The work he did for a living was often nothing more than grinding brake drums or cylinders, but it taught him the basics of precision machine-tool production he was to need later in life.

At this time, as early as 1924, he began thinking about a rotary engine and its many advantages in eliminating reciprocal actions if only the enormous problems of such a device could be solved. He continued to study by going to night schools and taking correspondence courses, but at least once in his early life, after some experimentation, he decided that the rotary idea could not be developed on a practical basis, although he continued to think about it.

To appreciate Wankel's long and successful career it is necessary to understand that engines and compressors are almost identical to each other except that they are reciprocal. An engine contains an expanding-gas situation and converts it to mechanical motion while a compressor receives mechanical motion and converts air or other gas to a high-pressure condition. Engines and compressors—like electric motors and generators—are similar in appearance and action except that they perform functions that are opposite to each other.

Much of Wankel's career, especially in its earlier periods, was taken up with the perfection of compressors rather than engines, both of which have similar problems, especially in the area of sealing. Wankel became, first, an expert in sealing problems, and he later applied his learning and experience to the rotary engine, since most of the rotary's problems were problems of sealing.

Wankel's first patent, taken out in 1929, dealt however with an engine with a reciprocating piston inside a horizontal cylinder. The cylinder had a combustion chamber at each end, and the piston was crowned at both ends. The piston had standard rings and contained no sealing innovations, so Wankel was aware that his first patented work was hardly an advancement toward the rotary he had had in mind for years. As an expert on seals he realized perhaps more than anyone else that great advances had to be made in sealing techniques before any kind of pure rotary could become a practicable reality.

He continued working with seals, devising many types of machines to test his ideas for applications to rotary engine principles. He determined early that the best arrangement would have to be a rotary piston that would drive the shaft while rotating around it. Sealing problems for such a setup were so complex, however, that after several years of further trying he had scored no success.

In 1933 Daimler-Benz began paying him to conduct research in his favorite fields, rotary engines and associated seals and valves. After about a year he switched to BMW to develop a piston engine with rotary valves. Here he was successful and soon received a patent for a sealing element he called a "packing body," a method of using a small low-friction surface for effective sealing without high spring force by utilizing combustion-gas pressure to keep the seal set against its mating surface.

By 1936 Wankel had obtained many sealing patents that in aggregate gave him complete coverage of the field of compressor, rotary valve, and internal-combustion engines in general. Two years before, he had applied for a patent on his first rotary engine, a two-rotor design with concentric, not eccentric, motion of the rotors. This engine was heavy, bulky, and complicated—typical of a first-generation design—and

56

worse than that, inefficient. It did, however, prove the worth of some of his recent ideas in sealing.

During this especially productive period of his life, Wankel became involved in exposing an embezzlement scheme perpetrated by the National-Socialist German Workers (Nazi) Party. When Adolf Hitler came to power, Wankel was thrown in jail for several months as a traitor to the party. When he was released in 1935 he moved from Heidelberg back to his hometown, Lahr. Within a year the Third Reich's air ministry called on him for technical help and Wankel soon found himself installed in his own institute, Wankel Versuchswerkstatten (WVW), in Lindau, Germany.

He started development work on a rotary-valve aircraft engine for Hermann Goering's Luftwaffe, assisted by Dip. Ing. ("certificated engineer") Wolf Dieter Bensinger, who headed the design and development of the Mercedes-Benz C-111 rotary engine more than thirty years later. Wankel did a great deal of aircraft-engine work, particularly in association with Daimler-Benz, in perfecting the great DB601 engine used in the Messerschmitt 109 fighter plane that became famous in World War II.

The Junkers company, another aircraft manufacturer, built and tested several experimental piston engines with Wankel rotary valves. A scheduled production run of one hundred engines for torpedo propulsion was prevented by Germany's surrender in 1945. For about a year after that, Wankel was imprisoned by the French occupation forces and his WVW institute was dismantled.

With the help of friends, Wankel was reestablished in 1951 in his own new technical center, the Technische Entwicklungsstelle, in Lindau am Bodensee, West Germany, on Lake Constance near the original site of his WVW. From this point, through twenty more years of hard work, the inventor's course was a straight one leading to a great fortune and world-wide fame. In December, 1969, he received an honorary doctorate from the Munich Technical Institute.

Shortly after opening his new technical center in 1951, Wankel signed the first of a long series of contracts with NSU, a prominent German manufacturer of motorcycles. The company was interested in Wankel's work on rotary valves and their possible application to a new line of motorcycle racing engines then under consideration. The valve work led to an experimental compressor to be used as a supercharger for motorcycle engines. Several Wankel compressors were built in 1954 that were considered highly successful. Wankel's complete seal grid, the culmination of many years of work on the problems of sealing, was used for the first time in these compressors, and the triangular rotor now famous in the Wankel engine was united with an epitrochoid-shaped housing.

As mentioned earlier, a compressor or air pump, given a spark ignition and a fuel charge, becomes an engine, and Wankel's work in the compressor field led quite naturally to the first rotary engine at NSU. The first DKM (for the German word *Drehkolbenmotor*, literally "rotary piston engine") was tested at NSU in 1957, but it ran only long enough to obtain a torque reading. It cracked up a few minutes after a difficult start, but it was historically the first Wankel rotary power plant.

Note that the DKM was concentric in the movement of its rotor. The first-generation engine, the DKM-54 (54 cubic centimeters in volume) was merely an experiment and was never meant to go into production—but it proved feasibility beyond doubt. The DKM was designed without regard to mounting in an automobile and connecting to a clutch and transmission, and so it had an outer housing that rotated.

It became the task of Dr. Walter Froede to design the KKM series (*Kreiskolbenmotor*, or "circuitous piston engine") in which the outer housing remained stationary. In Dr. Froede's version at NSU, the eccentric movement of the rotor (now accepted as standard in Wankel engines) was introduced. His first was the KKM-125, a single rotor unit, tested in 1957. It weighed only 37.4 pounds with a cast-iron housing and 23.2 pounds with an aluminum housing. A basic Wankel engine as we know it today, it had the sealing grid developed by Wankel, the chamber in epitrochoidal form, and triangular-rotor movement that was eccentric.

Inventions come about in as many ways as there are human personalities to create them. Some inventors are merely innovators who get a bright idea now and then and either drop it or allow it to pass on to others for purposes of perfection while busying themselves with startups of new and different projects. Edison personally supervised the perfection of the light bulb and personally threw the switch that lighted up the first city block to be electrically illuminated. He also brought us recorded sound, but literally thousands of people have been involved in removing the scratch and improving the fidelity to the point where a two dollar record surpasses the ability of the human ear to appreciate its full range of sound frequencies.

Fleming gave us the radio tube and Armstrong provided the basic circuits, but in today's transistorized world surely both of those geniuses would be happily amazed to see and hear the pocket radio any child can now buy at a five-and-dime. Yet these men had to do their thing first, to make possible the steps that followed.

Wankel's job was so difficult by comparison that he spent decades at it before his invention was in any condition to benefit from assistance from his colleagues. But finally, Wankel was ready for help, and development of his engine began to quicken its pace. This was accompanied, for the first time, by a sizable amount of favorable publicity, which led in due course to financial help for NSU via the selling of Wankel-engine licenses.

Wankel himself was a basic-idea man. He was much more interested in initiating primary principles as springboards for others than in participating in the follow-up detail work, such as building models and testing them, which he left to others. So at NSU his associates came to him frequently for consultation, then proceeded toward their separate objectives with minimal guidance.

The main principles were established. The engine, no matter what development course it took, must remain purely rotary with no reciprocating (up and down or back and forth) actions of any parts. Instead of creating a combustion chamber as a conventional piston does by starting, sliding in the cylinder, stopping, starting and sliding again, the function must be performed by a "rotary piston" that spins in a circle without interruption in its movement. This eliminates power losses associated with such reciprocal motion. Conventional valves, with their opening-closing stops and starts, are obviated also, since the triangular "piston" of the rotary engine needs only to pass by ports to achieve intake and permit exhaust. Vibration of conventional parts working in opposite directions need not be present in the rotary, and this should greatly increase engine life. Finally, with only one-third the number of parts found in a six-cylinder engine of comparable horsepower, the simpler structure of the rotary should make it quieter, more compact in size, and considerably lighter.

As you will see in Chapter 7, the comparatively simple construction of the Wankel involved extremely complicated machining to form the epitrochoidal "cylinder" in which the rotor revolves. And maintaining satisfactory contact between the rotor and its "cylinder wall"—as the piston rings seal their piston inside its cylinder in a conventional engine—proved to be an almost insurmountable task. There were lesser problems, lubrication, ignition, and combustion primarily, also to be solved. These problems had stopped all other engineers in their efforts to perfect what many of them felt to be, in theory at least, the ideal engine in rotary concept.

The DKM engine completed at NSU would have been difficult to mount in an automobile because the housing as well as the rotor inside it rotated. The KKM type, however, had a motionless housing with only the rotor moving internally, a

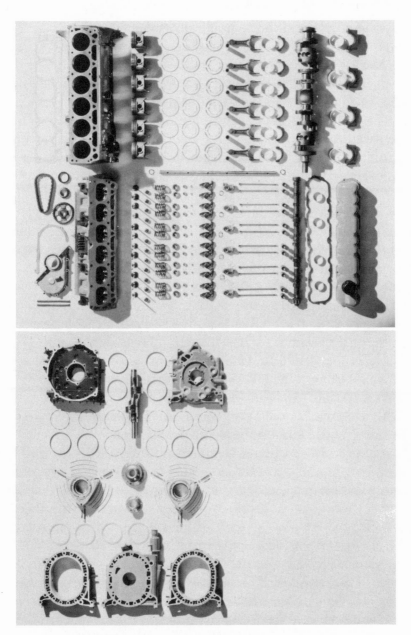

These pictures graphically demonstrate the difference in the number of parts in a conventional six-cylinder engine and a Mazda rotary engine of comparable horsepower.

marked advance toward a practical automobile power plant. In July 1959, endurance tests were begun on the KKM-250, and successful tests up to 1,000 hours were completed by the end of the year. The engine weighed a bit over forty-eight pounds and developed a peak horsepower of 44 at 9,000 rpm.

The endurance tests showed that the big problem, sealing, was well on its way toward a solution, and NSU decided to introduce the engine to the public in December 1959. The news went around the world with the speed of electronic broadcast and radiophoto, and engineers of all nationalities had the first important—and possibly revolutionary—device to discuss in many years. With wild speculation tempered by serious skepticism, discussion rose with renewed vigor following each subsequent announcement concerning the new little engine.

The year before, astute executives at Curtiss-Wright had caused their company to purchase the American rights to the Wankel engine from NSU. That license agreement was renegotiated in 1964 with various sharing of fees and royalties. On business outside North America, NSU would receive 54 percent of any income while Wankel would receive 36 percent and Curtiss-Wright 10 percent. On engines imported into the United States, the sharing was NSU 15 percent, Wankel 10 percent, and Curtiss-Wright 75 percent. In North America, manufactures by Curtiss-Wright would pay NSU-Wankel 1.5 percent if automotive, 3 percent if other. From entrance fees and royalties received by Curtiss-Wright for sublicensing, 60 percent would go to Curtiss-Wright, 24 percent to NSU, and 16 percent to Wankel—except engines exported to Germany, which would pay NSU 45 percent, Wankel 30 percent, and Curtiss-Wright 25 percent.

In 1965 Curtiss-Wright contracted with the Aerospace Electrical Division of Westinghouse Electric Corporation to develop a Wankel engine for a lightweight electricity generator set. The following year Curtiss-Wright sold a sublicense to Outboard Marine Corporation.

Following NSU's public announcement of the Wankel engine

in late 1959, officials of Toyo Kogyo Company, Limited, in Hiroshima, Japan, began to take an interest in the new development, which had previously received little attention in engineering circles, especially in the Far East. A manufacturer since 1920 of machine tools, championship motorcycles, three-wheel delivery cycles, subcompact autos, infantry rifles (before and during World War II), and, after the war, small cars and trucks, Toyo Kogyo was situated at the east end of Hiroshima, far enough from the epicenter of the atomic bomb blast of August 6, 1945, to escape with only window breakage and other minor damage.

Toyo Kogyo, mostly a light-truck builder in the years immediately following the war, reentered the passenger car field in 1960 with its low-cost R360 coupé. Early the same year public test-stand operations of the Wankel engine had been performed at a "rotary engine symposium" sponsored by the Verein Deutscher Ingenieure in Germany. When news of the engine reached Japan, Toyo Kogyo's engineering staff evinced immediate interest. From what little they were able to find out about the latest NSU engine, it was definitely superior to previous models, was the best so far developed by any company, and had good possibilities for practical use, at least in the small-car field, in which Toyo Kogyo was anxious to increase its share of the market. The company attempted to open talks with NSU pursuant to some sort of a licensing agreement for research, development, and manufacture of the Wankel in Japan, but the first query to NSU was curtly rebuffed. Toyo Kogyo later published the fact that the first response from NSU was "extremely conservative."

A few months later, on May 21, Toyo Kogyo was the luncheon host of the West German ambassador, Dr. Wilhelm Haas, during his visit to Hiroshima. Dr. Haas was treated to a tour of the well-laid-out plant, and during the meal that followed he expressed his appreciation for the hospitality he was receiving and asked whether there might be something he could do for the company in return. Discussion of the new

German rotary engine began, and company officials mentioned their disappointment with NSU's response and emphasized how anxious they were to talk serious business with the Germans. Up to this point NSU had received about a hundred queries similar to Toyo Kogyo's, a number of them coming from other Japanese companies. Toyo Kogyo's chances did not appear bright.

In July, however, the company received word through Ambassador Haas that it was invited to visit NSU with the idea of concluding a license agreement. Tsuneji Matsuda (pronounced something like "Mazda"), then president of Toyo Kogyo, departed in October with a party of five associates for a visit with NSU in West Germany. During their stay they observed bench tests of single-rotor engines in three sizes, 125, 250, and 400 cubic centimeters. With some distress they noted instability in all engines at idling speeds (then one of the most apparent problems). But at higher speeds the engines showed such smoothness that a coin could be stood on edge atop an engine during a run. This was impressive, and the Japanese were furthermore told that the two larger engines had already been mounted in the NSU Prinz sports cars and had covered 40,000 kilometers.

They may not have been told that the engines had a high breakdown rate, that they smoked terribly after a short term of use, and that metallurgical problems in sealing areas were far from solved. (The fact is that, several years later when NSU sold sports cars to the public—the Prinz and the Ro 80—the company had numerous complaints from customers. At the end of 1973 all the NSU cars on the road with rotary engines did not approach one year's production of Mazdas, and the Ro 80 had not yet been certified for sale in the United States.)

But negotiations proceeded apace and an agreement was concluded—not to cover the purchase of engines but for carrying on cooperative studies with the idea of bringing the engine to the market as soon as possible. The agreement was initialed on October 12 and ratified by the Japanese government the following July 4, 1961.

Immediately thereafter, a Toyo Kogyo party was sent to Germany for orientation—actually, to find out why the 250 and 400 engines, although road-tested, were not ready for production. The party found the engines still full of bugs, but they left with an agreement that they would be furnished technical information, including all necessary drawings and spare engines.

A development committee was formed at home and its conclusion was that the 400 engine offered the greatest possibilities. Such an engine, an NSU KKM-400, arrived in November, and the Hiroshima research group disassembled it, examined it, reassembled it, and put it on the test bench. It came up with an output of 43.8 hp at 9,000 rpm—surprising for such a small engine—but like its counterparts back in Germany, it had trouble at idle speeds.

Using only design drawings, Toyo Kogyo had already manufactured its own prototype No. 1 by the time the 400 arrived from Germany. The prototype showed excessive roughness at idle speeds, emitted clouds of smoke, and consumed oil at a rate beyond all practical use. Then at two hundred hours on the bench, its output of power suddenly dropped. When the crew dismantled the engine they discovered "chatter marks," signs of irregularity in the mating of the apex seals at each point of the triangular rotor with the inner lining of the housing, which meant that the electroplated lining was tearing up. This depressed the Japanese engineers and seemed to spell doom for their engine.

Early in 1962, after it was decided to mount an engine in a test car and check its adaptability to the road, other problems were discovered. Although the engine ran very smoothly at high speeds it continued to falter at idle, and upon deceleration strong vibrations built up.

Undaunted, the Toyo Kogyo engineering crew decided that, in view of the plans of the company for producing larger vehicles in the future, a two-rotor engine should be developed —this at a time when the single-rotor engine was proving most unsatisfactory and when even less technical data was available on a two-rotor concept!

In April 1963, the rotary engine development division of Toyo Kogyo was organized with four departments: research, design, testing, and materials research. With only five test benches to work on in an old gloomy building, conditions were recognized to be less than ideal, and plans went forward for construction of a new test laboratory.

By January 1964, the basic test cells were completed, a section of the lab that incorporated the most modern facilities and equipment. Endurance test cells followed, and these were put into operation at once. Computers and industrial television installed here were to play important roles in expediting research and development.

Each of the problems confronting development of the engine, it was decided, would be tackled at its base. Primary among these were the distressing chatter marks discovered in early testing. These are wave-like patterns that build up from vibration on contacting metal parts. They had been showing up on the trochoid surface where the apex seals rode. The closest counterpart in a piston engine would be cylinder scoring, a threat of early death to any engine and something that had to be eliminated before any hope could be expressed for the future development of the rotary.

The solution lay not in working on ordinary seal materials or treating the trochoid surface in any ordinary way. This, even if successful, would only postpone the problem, not prevent it. The procedure they adopted involved trying every possible material. Day in and day out, tests using every available substance were performed on the benches. Rotor housings, all with chatter marks, were soon heaped high in the laboratory, and nothing had worked.

The next decision then was to measure the particular vibrations that were causing the trouble and obtain data that could be quickly analyzed by the electronic computers recently installed in the lab. Six months of effort resulted in a conclusion to alter the basic configuration of the seals themselves. Proposed was a method of drilling a hole crosswise near the tip of the seal and then drilling another hole lengthwise to intersect with the first. The new apex seal, dubbed "cross hollow," proved to be satisfactory.

This was the first time anybody had made an apex seal that worked. Piston-ring technology was then more than one hundred years old and had enjoyed hundreds of technical generations of improvement. To accomplish in three years the breakthrough that the Japanese engineers achieved, virtually unassisted from the outside, was more than a miracle. It was incredible.

There was still, however, the serious problem of instability at low and idling speeds. This cannot be forgiven in any engine, because drivers have become accustomed to a smooth idle and find roughness supremely annoying; moreover, erratic motion damages engine mounts and shakes engine accessories loose, tears radiator hoses, and results in engine-stalling in traffic. Worse, misfiring fouls the combustion chambers and shortens spark plug life.

All earlier rotary engines had had peripheral ports (holes in the housing that acted as valves). The ports of the induction (breathing) system, therefore, were situated around the far-thest track followed by the rotors. After many experiments, the engineering staff came to suspect that this could be the basic cause of roughness. So in the next-generation engine the intake ports were moved to the side housings. (Same thing as reducing valve overlap in a piston engine.) The idea was to curtail the amount of combusted gases that was mixing with the newly inducted fuel charges. The educated guess was a good one. Stability at low speeds was established.

In spite of the victory over chatter marks, the company was not yet through with its work in the area of seals. The apex seal itself was too short-lived, and a new material had to be found that would better resist the severe conditions of wear suffered by the small seals that were positioned at the apexes of the triangular rotors. Research and experiment had shown that a nonmetal would offer the best wear-resistance, and from many such materials carbon was finally selected for tryouts.

A new research group connected with the materials research division was organized, and these people began technical work with a carbon supplier. As a result of numerous studies of carbonic materials, one was discovered that showed the minimal wear degradation of only a few tenths of a millimeter following a 1,000-hour continuous endurance test. This was comparable to an uninterrupted journey of more than two times around the earth at the equator at highway speeds, and was considered satisfactory.

When the German engines and the early Japanese models were bench-tested and later mounted in automobiles, quantities of white smoke issued from the exhaust system. This was not only intolerable from the air-pollution standpoint (by the mid-sixties already becoming a big issue), but it meant that the engines were consuming oil at an untenable rate and also fouling themselves internally. To the Japanese this appeared at first to be a minor mechanical problem (comparable to the need for a "ring job" in a piston engine) that could be handled in a hurry.

Like most of their other problems, it turned out differently. The Germans had been wrestling with the phenomenon from the beginning too, and they finally arrived at a solution—for the NSU. But it could not be borrowed for application on the Toyo Kogyo because of some basic structural differences. However, in due course, shortly before the first Mazda cars were scheduled to be put on the market, the Japanese crew worked out their problems and the smoking ceased.

Finally, there was gear trouble inside the engine that had to be eliminated. Gears inside a piston engine are low-load simple things for driving subassemblies such as the distributor and the camshaft. On the rotary, however, with its rotors following

68

the epitrochoidal inside surface via an eccentric motion around the mainshaft, gears provide all-important phasing. Many engines on test failed in wild fits when these vital gears tore apart.

To solve this problem the Toyo Kogyo engineers performed many series of complicated electronic measurements of the special forces impressed on the engine gears. Their work resulted in a whole new theory of energy-transfer forces, proper application of which eventually brought normal longevity to the gearing system.

In 1967 Toyo Kogyo brought out its first rotary-engine car for public sale, the Cosmo Sports, better known as the Mazda 110S. The next year the Familia Rotary Coupé (Mazda R100 Coupé) was offered to the public. In 1969, the 3-millionth Mazda vehicle (including only a few with rotary engines) came off the assembly lines of Toyo Kogyo. By this time, full-scale export of rotary-engine cars was under way, principally to nations in the Far East.

The following year, 1970, the first rotary engines ever offered for sale in the United States were in Mazda automobiles. In that entire year exactly 649 autos with rotary engines were put on the road here. Had these been General Motors engines in full production, they could have been produced in less than an hour.

## With All the World Watching

The brilliant $2 million purchase by Curtiss-Wright of the American rights to the Wankel engine from NSU Motorenwerke AG in 1958 was the first chapter in what could be called the "American phase" of the Wankel engine story. Yet it was Toyo Kogyo, twelve years later, that furnished Americans with the first production car, the Mazda, that mounted a Wankel rotary engine.

In the years from 1958 to the present, however, Curtiss-Wright, the famous aircraft and aircraft-engine manufacturer, contributed greatly toward the research and development of rotaries of all sorts, particularly in the stationary-electricity-generation, watercraft, aircraft, and snowmobile fields.

A development contract with Westinghouse resulted in power generation equipment of light weight, mobility, dependability, and comparatively low fuel consumption. Primarily designed for low fuel consumption in military uses where resupply of fuel can be a problem, the generator set is intended for forward combat-area applications of radar, missile launchers, radio and television communications, airstrip landing lights, and other military and naval needs.

A Curtiss-Wright sublicense to Outboard Marine Corporation in 1966 resulted, in only about five years, in the development of sophisticated Johnson and Evinrude rotary engines for snowmobiles and motorboats. The first Outboard Marine rotary engines for snowmobiles were marketed in 1972, making OMC the first American company to design, manufacture, and *market* a Wankel engine.

OMC's rotary-engine decision was crystallized at an engineering product demonstration for high-level management at a secluded Wisconsin lake in the summer of 1964. The meeting's purpose was to review research programs on marine gas-turbine engines and an early Curtiss-Wright Wankel. The gas turbine then was being seriously considered by American auto manufacturers and its future looked bright. But at this demonstration meeting, the Wankel presented qualities equaling the turbine without the expenses of exotic steels, high revolutions-per-minute, and bulky, complicated heat exchangers. Management, according to S. L. Metcalf, director of marine

71

engineering, did a complete about-face, shelved the turbine, and took up the cause of the Wankel for several of their ongoing engine programs.

The 1966 license agreement with Curtiss-Wright and the German licensor then called NSU-Wankel allowed OMC to develop, manufacture, and sell what they now call RC (rotary-combustion) engines in the marine and snowmobile fields. OMC started with snowmobiles, although at the time there was much speculation among its own engineers as to which of its products the RC engine should be applied first. Many were the technical difficulties to be overcome before designs could be refined to be competitive in performance, durability, and cost, compared to other OMC engines with which the company had had a head start of fifty years. The snowmobile was chosen for the first application because the requirements for ruggedness in that field were the greatest among all the OMC product lines. The company wanted to field-test its new RC under rigorous conditions over the wide range of speeds, loads, and temperatures that a snowmobile application could provide. After all, a snowmobiler, like no other driver, can run at full throttle for hours in deep snow at low speed or, on the other hand, can career down a mountain slope at runaway rpm's—and do this at sub-zero or mild temperatures and at all altitudes. Nothing compares with the snowmobile for engine testing.

OMC was conservative in its development work and spent no less than nine years on the process of bringing the engine to the point of announcement. Part of the long development time was consumed in perfecting a tungsten-carbide coating for its engine's "cylinder walls," the inner lining of the rotor housing. This type of lining, which cost five dollars per square inch, is not considered essential for less heavy-duty applications such as automotive.

In early 1973, Charles D. Strang, group vice president in charge of marine products for OMC, announced that his company had been "diligently pursuing the design and development of RC outboard motors." But he cautioned that even

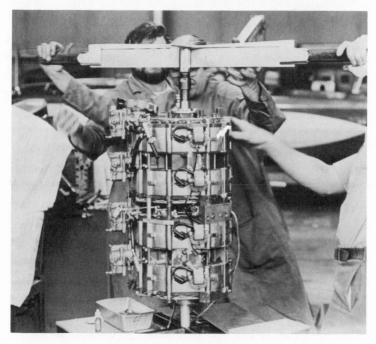

The world's most powerful outboard engine, a four-rotor Wankel, was developed for installation in this Outboard Marine Corporation experimental racing boat.

Experimental Outboard Marine Corporation Wankel engine for boat racing is of modular construction, allowing it to be adapted to perform as a single-, double-, triple-, or, as in this case, a four-rotor outboard powerplant.

though his company was at the point of field (on-the-water) testing—which of necessity must be done in the public eye—OMC was nowhere near the marketing point for outboard engines.

He admitted that his company put snowmobile engines on the market less than one year after fielding the experimental machines, but he cautioned that outboards were quite a different matter. He added that while he could not say when Johnson and Evinrude outboards would be marketed, he could say with assurance that it would *not* be in 1974. Then he announced a racing program designed to speed up the laboratory development of the new RC outboard line of engines.

The engine ready for racing was a four-rotor, high-output, charge-cooled package with lightweight all-aluminum construction. With a displacement of approximately two liters, the unusual engine was cooled internally by the fuel-air mixture flowing from the carburetor to the combustion chamber and externally by water scooped from just below the race-course surface. The four housings containing the rotors were stacked one upon the other, and the rotary racing engine displayed about two-thirds more horsepower and torque than OMC had ever seen in its best high-performance engines of the piston type.

This special hand-built power plant was designed specifically with future outboard motors in mind. Its modular construction could be readily adapted to a selection of power sizes, from a single-rotor concept to a combination of two or more rotors, using the same sets of parts.

In September of 1973 OMC announced a breakthrough in the formerly expensive coating of the housing raceway. The coating, a mixture of tungsten carbide and a nickel aluminide material, is supplied by Metro, Inc., Westbury, New York, in a powder form and is applied to the cast-aluminum raceway by a plasma flame-spray system. The innovation, to provide a vital wear-resistant lining to this type of high-speed outboard engine, reduced the cost of the lining from five dollars to only a

74

few cents per square inch in the racing prototype engine, which has four rotors, each with an inner surface of 77 square inches. Future engines for the public will be produced in smaller sizes, some having only one rotor and others two or more, depending on the horsepower requirement for the many sizes and types of watercraft. Thousands of hours were invested by OMC and Metro in developing just this application method, but it was important in reducing the price of the engine to a practical range before offering the engine to the public.

Much has been said about Toyo Kogyo's achievement in perfecting a road-ready Wankel-engine automobile for world-wide sales and in being the first auto manufacturer to offer such a car to the American public. While the relatively small Japanese company was actively performing bench and proving-ground tests—which could hardly be kept secret—most major car makers of the world were at least "looking into" the matter.

It should be emphasized that all auto manufacturers have large research and development departments in which many different kinds of possibilities, both within and without the auto field, are under investigation. Management makes the ultimate decisions as to what courses are to be pursued beyond certain points, of course, and sometimes management actually initiates research, especially if it is inspired by sales, pro-duction, or other economic factors.

So in the early 1960s, and in a few cases even before that time, there had been conversations regarding the Wankel in all the companies' conference rooms. Whether, and how far, each company decided to go into Wankel research became matters of individual interpretations of the situation insofar as it could be foreseen from each firm's point of view. Because the American auto manufacturers are in fierce competition with each other and with many of the foreign car makers as well, they seldom do things the same way and never act in concert except when ordered to do so by the government, as in certain safety matters.

75

The various corporations are structured differently, and in many cases top-level management decisions are the results of highly individual thought. In spite of this, the final products from the various companies often show distressingly close similarities. Horsepower-to-weight ratios, for example, may be almost identical among a number of models that cross company lines. This is understandable: research is continuously done by all the firms producing automobiles in an attempt to sample the public taste in such matters, and if such surveys are accurate they will provide the same indications.

The vast majority of Americans, including many who won't admit it, want lots of power under the hood. They have been told that power can become a safety factor in a tight situation, but that's only a minor contributor to the public's desire for such power. Major contributors have been the many auto races that have been held since the infancy of the automobile and that have established power (which translates to speed) as an almost undeniable essential of engine quality.

Another major factor is the American's basic competitive instinct (not unknown among Europeans and Orientals but definitely more pronounced in North America). When an American or a Canadian wants to pass someone on the highway, it becomes an urgent, if unconscious, need.

So we have powerful engines that can propel our cars at high speeds and with rapid acceleration. The car makers put even more time, effort, and money into styling, in view of the fact that women hold some 52 million of the 118 million driver licenses in the nation. When the surveys go out they come back showing the same preferences. Little wonder that our cars look and act alike regardless of brand. There are exceptions, of course (Gremlin, Corvette, Charger, Opel GT), but it's not usual to find them near the top of the best-seller lists.

When a manufacturing executive is confronted with a change, he resists it because being different is not good business. This theory has been tested over and over. The

Chrysler Airflow of the early 1930s is a classic example of an otherwise excellent venture that failed for this reason.

But the Wankel could not be ignored. And General Motors, the world's largest manufacturing corporation, in this case may have been the only firm able to take the risk. American Motors, the smallest of the American Big Four, simply could not undertake a revolutionary engine change. Its board of directors is composed of brilliant, conservative individuals who must protect the relatively small treasury of their presently prosperous factory at all costs. When a major slip could be disastrous, the wait-and-see attitude is the only one that makes sense, and that's exactly the position AMC finds itself in today.

"If the Wankel is a success in the marketplace, we can always start by buying it from another manufacturer," a company spokesman said when asked about his firm's plans for the future.

Chrysler, much larger than AMC, has a more complicated problem. To tool for the amount of Wankel production that would be required if Chrysler were to take such an engine to market would probably preclude all other tooling—the commitment to the Wankel would be a drastic move on the part of management. So several years ago Chrysler started what could only be called a "negative advertising" campaign—not in actual advertising pages or electronic-media spots (that would be too difficult to retract later), but in public declarations to the press by top company officials, to the effect that the Wankel is a bad engine.

"The Wankel rotary engine will turn out to be one of the most unbelievable fantasies ever to hit the world auto industry," said Alan G. Loofbourrow, vice-president in charge of engineering and research for Chrysler Corporation, in July of 1972. Admitting that the Wankel "has caught the public fancy as few things have," he added: "That is its biggest asset at the moment—its novelty. But novelty is not enough."

At a time when many other auto engineers and industry

analysts had been predicting that the rotary engine will replace the conventional engine in this decade, his note of pessimism was a jarring one. Loofbourrow brought up a point seldom heard, that there will be sales problems if people have to pay more for the engine and have to get it serviced more often. This sounded strange at a time when conventional engines were at their highest price in history due to inflation and constant adding-on of anti-pollution devices, and at a time when customer dissatisfaction with the new balky piston engines was at an all-time high.

He brought out the old engineer's axiom that, after all, a six-cylinder piston engine was smooth, too, although few are sold now compared to V-8's and in-line fours. He said, "A Wankel that is not balanced is rough as a cob. People think that a rotary engine is inherently smooth, but if it's not balanced it's going to be rough." He neglected to say that that's true with any engine, that all engines are balanced when they leave the factory, and that the Wankel is the easiest of all engines to balance because of its small number of moving parts, their simplicity, and the fact of no reciprocating actions inside the engine itself.

He said there is a tough problem with emissions "because [the Wankel] is basically a dirty engine. Today, just to meet the California standards, it needs two black boxes [miniature computers] and two dual-exhaust reactor systems." He could not have known in 1972 that a year later, in 1973, the Mazda-with-Wankel would have an exhaust clean enough, thanks to those computers and reactors, to pass not only the stringent 1975 but also the even more stringent 1976 federal emission standards.

"There is a spark plug problem of some kind," he continued. "We have been testing Mazdas, and keeping them from backfiring is a chore. The first one started backfiring at under 3,000 miles." Perhaps his research department should have hired a Mazda tune-up technician. One brand-new Mazda RX-3 with stick-shift tested by the author backfired once or twice a

78

day at first but was easily adjusted, and now at 4,000 miles it still does not backfire. Another car driven by the author, an RX-2 with automatic transmission, did not backfire during the time he drove it, from a 1,000-mile odometer reading to about 1,600 miles.

"As for economy," Loofbourrow went on, "you have a built-in headwind with the Wankel. It uses between 5 and 15 percent more fuel for equivalent performance. You have to put more gas in to do the same job, and this is a pretty fundamental thing." Here he had a point. The Mazdas-with-Wankel do not have a fuel-consumption rate to brag about. With automatic transmission and air conditioning, the driver cannot expect to get much better than 16.5 mpg on the highway, and with a stick-shift and no air conditioning the economy does not improve much above 22 mpg. This is not good for a car that weighs just a bit over a ton, but there's another consideration. The fuel mileages quoted above in nonprofessional, average-driver motoring are for Mazda rotary engines that qualify, without mileage-reducing modifications or added parts, under the 1976 interim NOx emission regulations. Other small cars with better fuel mileages in 1973 may be considerably degraded in fuel consumption before reaching qualification. The ability of the rotary engine to use low-octane fuel may help, especially in near-future years, to offset its slightly lower mpg economy.

"The torque curve is different; it's a different ball game the way it uses performance," Loofbourrow offered as his final complaint. And he was right. But his criticism is relevant mostly where an automatic transmission is used. The Mazda with automatic transmission (manufactured by Japan Automatic Transmission Company, owned approximately one-third each by Toyo Kogyo, the Mazda maker, Nissan, maker of the Datsun, and Ford) does not perform like the Mazda with stick-shift. The nature of the rotary engine results in a slower acceleration at slow engine speeds, with the engine gaining much more rapidly at higher speeds. So, pulling away from the curb, the driver does not have the instant acceleration of a piston engine. A governor inside every automatic transmission determines the speed at which each shift occurs, depending on the amount of depression of the accelerator pedal. Toyo Kogyo engineers elected to cause their automatic transmission to shift quickly, before engine speed reaches the point of rapid acceleration, but this is adjustable within certain limits.

Meanwhile the Mazda retains a quality long sought after and not available in the smaller piston engines: the ability to provide better and better acceleration at higher engine speeds. In a piston engine, volumetric efficiency begins to fall off in the mid-range of cruising speed, so that with a small engine it could be dangerous to try to pass a car that is going, say, 65 mph. In the Mazda, however, the engine is just approaching its maximum torque when highway speeds are reached, and its pickup at 60, 65, or 70 is nothing short of phenomenal. This may not be a help to drivers who stay at slow traffic speeds much of the time, but it is a boon for highway drivers.

At the end of the press conference reported in the Detroit *News* of July 6, 1972, Loofbourrow mentioned that "the door is still open" for Chrysler on a Wankel license. "Anybody," he said, "can get a license who wants to pay the money."

There was a feeling then and later that Loofbourrow's words had come not from his engineering department but instead from the marketing end of Chrysler, which is obviously caught between a rock and a hard place in its wait-and-see attitude. This attitude is unusual for Chrysler, with an engineering department considered by many observers to be the most progressive of the Big Four.

Henry Ford II said in 1972 that the rotary probably won't replace the piston in "my lifetime." Jan Norbye, automotive editor of *Popular Science* and the author of *The Wankel Engine: Design, Development, Applications*, said, "Ford is caught with its pants down." In 1971 Ford made attempts to acquire 20 percent of Toyo Kogyo. While negotiations were under way, however, the sales of Mazdas in the United States soared and the deal turned sour. In 1972 Toyo Kogyo's new president, Kohei Matsuda, offered Ford 20 percent of everything *but* the company's rotary developments. A Ford spokesman put it this way: "The Japanese left us standing at the altar."

Reliable estimates put the cost of a Ford changeover to rotary at $1 billion. It would cost GM twice that amount but GM's profits are three times that of Ford. The holders of the Wankel patents, NSU, the Wankel company, and Curtiss-Wright, would want a down payment of $30 million to $50 million for American manufacturing rights plus a minimum 4 percent royalty (about ten dollars per engine). Ford could handle that, but if the rotary were short-lived and Ford had to retool again in the 1980s, it would hurt Ford much more than GM.

So Ford continues to defer production plans and fall further behind GM while shopping for 15,000 to 20,000 rotaries as options for the 1975 or 1976 Capri, Maverick, Mustang, or Pinto. There are only two sources: the new Comotor engine plant in West Germany that is owned jointly by Audi NSU and Citroen, where the Wankel price is double that of comparable piston engines, and Toyo Kogyo, which isn't interested in selling any engines to outsiders before 1975 at the earliest.

Ford's Ford-Werke AG of West Germany still holds a three-year license to make rotaries there. But if Ford tried to import them into the United States, Curtiss-Wright would almost certainly demand royalties. So the expectation is that Ford will try to buy a U.S. license soon. But the last word from Henry Ford himself (September, 1972) was: "We are not negotiating and we have no plans to do so." The same Henry Ford also once stated publicly, many years ago, that his company would not manufacture small cars.

In 1969 and early 1970 rumors increased on the subject of GM's interest in the Wankel engine—increased to the point of urgent press inquiries. To curtail the then-rampant speculation about what the great manufacturer could and would do if it should suddenly take an interest in buying out one of the

81

several smaller companies that already held licenses, GM said only that it was "holding discussions" with Wankel G.m.b.H. Dr. Wankel had built the first operating rotary engine in 1957 in conjunction with the motorcycle and small-car maker, NSU, a German corporation that had been in a shaky financial condition for several years previously. Wankel's basic design was modified and improved by a close associate at NSU, Dr. Walter Froede. Later, with Ernest Hutzenlaub, an inventor and financier who put up $250,000 for further engine development, Wankel formed a fifty-fifty partnership called Wankel G.m.b.H.

Curtiss-Wright was NSU's first license customer. With a shrewd and farsighted investment of $2 million, Curtiss-Wright not only received the right to build the engine itself but it also won control of licensing rights for North America, and in a subsequent renegotiation, a share of world-wide royalties.

NSU's manufacturing business continued to stagger and in 1969 it merged into Auto Union, a subsidiary of mighty Volkswagen. However, in the merger deal, VW had to give up most of the potential Wankel profits and turn them over to NSU's original shareholders by issuing them profit-sharing certificates called *Genussscheine*.

Today the main ownership of Wankel rotary patent rights is divided among VW, which pays out the royalty money to the former NSU holders, and Curtiss-Wright, and Wankel G.m.b.H. The complicated formula for dividing royalty revenue was mentioned earlier. Interestingly, Wankel isn't Wankel any more. Wankel and Hutzenlaub sold their partnership in 1971 for $30 million to Lonrho, Ltd., a British holding company. Dr. Wankel, seventy-one in 1974, leads a prosperous life of active research, busying himself with contract work on various development projects involving the Wankel engine.

After GM confirmed its serious negotiations on June 1, 1970 with Wankel G.m.b.H., industry reports from Frankfurt, Germany detailed the information that GM desired to acquire 40 percent of Wankel G.m.b.H. and had offered, through its West

82

German subsidiary, Adam Opel AG, about $27.5 million for those shares. Obviously, this would have brought GM into all present and future licensing agreements. The official word from GM at that time was to the effect that "discussions are being held with Wankel as part of our policy of investigating all possible automotive sources."

GM officials didn't get the bargain they were dickering for, but they came up with a better—and more expensive—deal than had ever been made on the Wankel, and even at its high price it may turn out to be a bargain unique in automotive history. On November 2, 1970 GM issued a press release that said in part:

> General Motors has agreed to enter into a worldwide, nonexclusive, paid-up license agreement with Audi-NSU, Wankel G.m.b.H., and Curtiss-Wright to facilitate its further intensive research and development studies of the Wankel rotary combustion engine to determine whether it is suitable for GM automotive applications.

The release cautioned that the agreement was subject to approval of managements of the participating companies on or before December 31, 1970 and stated that it covered the manufacture and sale by GM of the Wankel rotary-combustion engine except as it applies to aircraft propulsion. (From that time forward the name Wankel was dropped by GM, which now refers to the engine as its "rotary-combustion (RC)" engine. This is interesting in view of the fact that GM never worried about the name Diesel being applied to its famous line of "Jimmy" diesel engines and in fact named one of its most important divisions Detroit Diesel. But there is an interesting pattern here: When Chrysler beat GM to the market with its "alternator," GM followed with its "alternating current generator," in spite of the fact that the last word generally refers to the older style six-volt dynamo which was replaced by a twelve-volt type in all American automobiles.)

The tab for GM on the Wankel deal was a prodigious one,

and it will take the American buying public a number of years to pay it: $50 million, paid as a $5 million down payment at the end of 1970, four following year-end payments of $10 million each, and a final $5 million payment at the end of 1975. There was a cautious provision that allowed GM to abrogate the deal, on one day's notice, by not making any one of the year-end payments, but that isn't likely to happen, and as of 1974 GM has paid a total of $35 million while getting its RC engine ready for production.

In 1972, when the GM RC project was in full swing under the leadership of Robert Templin, one of the world's most respected engineers, things were going smoothly at the GM Technical Center at Warren, Michigan. Among the several hundred personnel assigned to the project morale was high and some were talking. There was word that a 145-hp rotary would be introduced on a 1974 Vega GT and that a year later the GM RC would be in its own front-wheel-drive "Super Vega."

This led to much speculation in the press, and GM officials, aware that if a few hundred thousand potential customers decided to "wait another year" for a car with a rotary engine, chaos in the market could result, put the clamps on any further leaking of information. GM executives said in 1972 and early 1973 that they didn't know what they were going to do about their rotary, let alone when.

Dr. David E. Cole, professor of mechanical engineering at the University of Michigan, told a Wankel seminar at Traverse City, Michigan, in early August, 1973, that the rotary engine will bear out its original billing as a "revolutionary advancement in automotive powerplants." Dr. Cole is the son of Edward N. Cole, president of GM, who also spoke at the seminar. The senior Cole listed four basic advantages of the RC and said its full potential can be realized only when a total vehicle can be designed around it.

"The engine is as much as 50 percent smaller than a comparable piston engine, giving it a high power-to-bulk ratio," he said, adding, "It is about 30 percent lighter, giving it

**84**

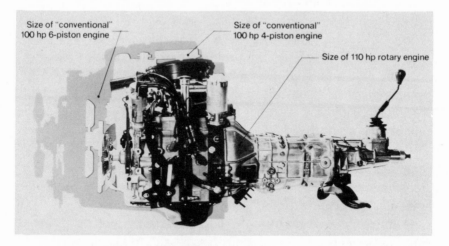

Size of "conventional" 100 hp 6-piston engine

Size of "conventional" 100 hp 4-piston engine

Size of 110 hp rotary engine

The large gray outline represents the size of a conventional six-cylinder engine, the white outline is of a four-cylinder engine, and the smallest engine is a two-rotor Mazda rotary of comparable horsepower but more compact configuration.

a high power-to-weight ratio. Third, it has about 40 percent fewer major components and is extremely smooth and quiet. And finally, because of its reduced size and weight for power, it gives the car designer new appearance and packaging opportunities."

Dr. Cole, a top world expert on the Wankel, talked about the intricate and sophisticated problems of the engine's sealing system and admitted that Mazda and NSU had apparently managed those problems successfully. The younger Cole had recently visited Dr. Wankel in Germany, and they had talked about the oft-touted fuel-consumption problems of the RC.

"In fact," Cole told the seminar, "90 percent of the rotary engine's fuel economy difficulty can be managed through improvements in sealing technology rather than through engine-design modifications."

Admitting that extremely hot exhaust gases have been another serious problem, the professor said, "This may prove to be a blessing in disguise for pollution control." He explained that the high-temperature exhaust gases cause durability problems for the exhaust ports but may in fact allow easier control of emissions by thermal reactors, which work more quickly and efficiently at high temperatures. This is something that Toyo Kogyo discovered some time ago, and Mazda cars, because of their thermal reactors, have been able to qualify under the 1975 and 1976 emission standards of the federal government. More on this in Chapter 7.

As this book goes to press, the latest official announcement from GM occurred at the Traverse City seminar, and it came from the mouth of GM's president. Edward N. Cole stated that GM will produce 100,000 Wankel-powered Vegas, "starting in 1974." Other reliable GM sources bumped the figure up to a possible 200,000. Given a movable timetable to deal with possible strikes or supply difficulties, they generally agreed that "announcement" will take place in August 1974 to cover the new 1975 Vega equipped with a Wankel engine. It is possible—in fact, likely—that many more than 100,000 GM RC engines will find themselves in American-built cars in the 1975-model year. The figure of 100,000 is not a large one for General Motors, which builds about 20,000 engines of all kinds per day when it is in full production. The pressure from Mazda's rapidly increasing dealer organization and resulting sales is enormous. GM will get with it on the fastest possible accelerating scale, you can be sure.

What then happens to Mazda? Toyo Kogyo has a good five-year head start, and when a GM RC comes on the market, says C. R. Brown, general manager of Mazda of America, "It can only help us."

# 7 Inside the Wonderful World of Wankel

In order for an engine to be revolutionary it must depart completely from previous concepts, designs, and engineering principles. And to be both revolutionary and successful it must find a place in the mechanical world where it is useful and in some ways more valuable than its predecessors.

The truck manufacturing industry had an engine revolution of sorts in the 1930s when the diesel, a similar piston-type engine, began to take over from the "gas burners"—and it may be on the verge of a real revolution if the gas turbine proves out in the next few years as it is expected to do. The aircraft industry experienced a genuine engine revolution when it changed over from pistons to turboprop and pure-jet power-plants, both versions of the gas turbine.

But until the Wankel, no engine ever threatened even to approach the position of dominance in automobile propulsion held by the piston. Both the Wankel and the piston are internal-combustion engines, with intake, compression, com-bustion, and exhaust episodes in each cycle. But there the similarity ends.

The piston engine is so-called because each of its cylinders contains a piston connected by a rod to its crankshaft. The automobile piston engine is a four-stroke-cycle type, with each combustion chamber taking in a mixture of gasoline and air in vapor form as each piston travels its first down-stroke in the cylinder, being pulled by the crankshaft. The fuel mixture is inducted via the intake valve for that cylinder. At the bottom end of the first piston stroke (bottom dead center), the intake valve is allowed to snap shut—valve movement is timed by the camshaft, which is geared to the crankshaft. With the intake valve shut, the piston reaches bottom, stops, and begins to travel upwards as it is pushed by the crankshaft. As the piston moves up on this compression stroke, the maximum combus-tion-chamber volume of, say, $8\frac{1}{2}$ is reduced to minimum, say, 1. Such an engine would be said to have a compression ratio of $8\frac{1}{2}$ to 1, a common ratio found in late-model engines.

At the time the piston reaches top dead center, compression is at maximum (about two hundred pounds per square inch) and the gasoline vapor, now intimately rammed against the oxygen in the compressed air, is fuel with more power than dynamite or even TNT. But it is not an explosive in the usual sense of the word—it does not normally detonate like dynamite, although it can and will if abused. At the point of top dead center an electric current with a pressure of about 22,000 volts is supplied, and the current jumps the gap of the spark plug, causing ignition.

For proper timing of ignition in certain types of automobile engines, the spark is often supplied slightly before the piston reaches top dead center. This is because the fuel-burning is not instantaneous and must be given some time to get started. So the spark is supplied 2, 5, or even as much as 10 degrees (of crankshaft rotation) early, so that by the time the piston reaches top dead center and starts its important power stroke downwards, the flame is well under way.

When ignition occurs, a flame-front develops at the spark plug and works its way outward in all directions. The flame-front gradually changes the fuel charge to a rapidly expanding gas that builds up a pressure several times greater than the compression pressure. It is this combustion pressure that runs the engine and propels the automobile. As the pressure pushes the piston downwards on the combustion, or power, stroke, the heat-energy developed in the combustion chamber is carried by the connecting rod to the crankshaft. This power stroke is, therefore, the only one of the four strokes in the cycle that contributes to horsepower output of the engine.

At or near the bottom of the power stroke, while combustion pressure is still building, the exhaust valve is opened by the camshaft, and whatever combustion power remains blows rapidly through the valve with a loud "pop" that must be silenced in the exhaust system by means of the muffler and associated pipes.

Now, beginning at bottom dead center, the piston is pushed by the crankshaft to the top of the cylinder again, and with the exhaust valve open, most of the remainder of the combustion product is cleared from the combustion chamber. Unfortunately, there is never time in the latter two strokes of the four-stroke cycle for the fuel to complete its burning process.

Fire passes through the exhaust valve and into the manifold. The major problem engineers are contending with today is management of that still-burning exhaust product.

Gasoline is a complicated compound of hydrogen and carbon, a hydrocarbon, to which a small amount of tetraethyl lead is usually added for purposes of proper combustion. By itself in liquid form it will not burn, or oxidize, because of oxygen insufficiency. (A can or tank of gasoline is easily ignited, however, because gasoline readily vaporizes in the presence of air, and it is the vapor that first ignites, resulting in heat that rapidly vaporizes more gasoline, providing more fuel, and so on.) [The carburetor takes in air and is supplied with liquid gasoline, which it vaporizes to form a fuel of the correct air-gasoline mixture to be taken into the engine.]

The hydrogen (not the carbon) in the gasoline and the oxygen (not the nitrogen and trace elements) in the air, when combined in the combustion process, are the actual elements of the fuel. Combustion products that result in the exhaust are water, carbon dioxide, unburned hydrocarbons, carbon monoxide, and certain oxides of nitrogen. Dismissing for the moment a few lead-compound particulates from the anti-knock additive and a few insignificant trace elements, the primary concerns of anti-pollution-oriented engineers are the emissions of unburned hydrocarbons, carbon monoxide, and oxides of nitrogen in the exhaust product, because all of these are toxic to humans, plants, and animals.

Unburned hydrocarbons result from incomplete combustion; carbon monoxide results from a too-rich fuel mixture and also from incomplete combustion. The former can be handled by various methods of completing the combustion process (in the Mazda rotary engine, a thermal reactor is employed), and the latter can be handled by better carburetion and more critical spark timing.

Oxides of nitrogen are developed in the combustion process itself, and they are much more difficult to handle. For the next few years, at least, they will have to be handled in most cars by

**91**

means of catalytic conversion, in which, in a special muffler-like device, the gases are passed through a sort of filter containing platinum or other rare metal and are converted by the metal catalyst to harmless substances.

It is significant that the Wankel engine emits unburned hydrocarbons and carbon monoxide in quantities similar to those from a piston engine—and these are easily oxidized by a thermal reactor—but, because of lower combustion temperatures (explained later), it tends to emit lower quantities of oxides of nitrogen. The fact of the lower oxides-of-nitrogen emission is presently one of the most important considerations in any comparison of the piston engine with the Wankel.

The operation of the piston engine is familiar to all mechanically minded persons and not difficult for anyone to understand. The piston merely moves up and down in the cylinder, with four strokes involved in completing each combustion cycle. The other three, five, or seven cylinders (depending on the kind of engine) perform identical functions in turn and with sufficient rapidity to provide a steady source of power.

In the Wankel, the same internal-combustion process is accomplished, but in an entirely different way and with somewhat different results. Instead of pistons-in-cylinders, rotors-in-housings are used. The rotors are roughly triangular in shape and they turn inside specially shaped raceways that have been machined on the internal surfaces of the housings.

Now if the rotors were merely to spin inside a cylindrical housing, in the way an electric motor's armature turns inside its stator, there would be no engine, because the four episodes of the combustion cycle would not be possible and work could not be performed. But the rotor (there are two in the Mazda engine) describes two concurrent movements: it spins like a motor armature and simultaneously travels an eccentric path to follow the epitrochoidal configuration of the inside surface of the housing. It not only spins around its shaft but—because its shaft is eccentric—moves inside the housing in a simultane-

92

**1. Intake.**
Fuel/air mixture is drawn into combustion chamber by revolving rotor through intake port (upper left). No valves or valve-operating mechanism needed.

**2. Compression.**
As rotor continues revolving, it reduces space in chamber containing fuel and air. This compresses mixture.

**3. Ignition.**
Fuel/air mixture now fully compressed. Leading sparkplug fires. A split-second later, following plug fires to assure complete combustion.

**4. Exhaust.**
Exploding mixture drives rotor, providing power. Rotor then expels gases through exhaust port.

**1. Intake.**

**2. Compression.**

**3. Ignition.**

**4. Exhaust.**

Comparison of how the four episodes of intake, compression, ignition-power, and exhaust take place in a Mazda Wankel rotary engine and in a conventional piston-in-cylinder engine.

ous but eccentric pattern. This will become clear in an observance of the four-episode combustion cycle.

⌡ The rotary engine begins its intake of the gasoline-air mixture when the rotor passes over a port in the side of the housing at a time when there is only a small-volume area between the rotor and its housing. As the rotor continues to move, the volume of that area increases rapidly as the rotor, while spinning, moves away from the port. This compares to the first downstroke of a piston. The increase in volume of the chamber causes suction that brings the fuel charge into the engine.

Following induction of the fuel charge, the next apex (point) of the rotor covers the intake port, and the spinning-plus-eccentric movement of the rotor begins to decrease the volume of what is about to become the combustion chamber, compressing the fuel mixture.

By the time the mixture is fully compressed the portion of the rotor now being considered has moved to the area of the raceway where ignition is to take place and where, on the Mazda engine, there are two spark plugs, called "leading" and "trailing." The leading plug is the first one encountered by the compressing portion of the rotor. It fires, initiating the flame front, and then the trailing plug fires to assist in the combustion of this particular fuel charge.

The rotor continues to spin, and as it does its also-eccentric movement allows the fired and rapidly expanding combustion gases to drive it away from the raceway. From the instant of ignition until the apex reaches the exhaust port, power is developed in the engine.

When the exhaust port is reached, however, the continuing combustion "pops" through the port and becomes the leading portion of the exhaust. The following apex of the rotor, in its continuing movement toward the exhaust port, clears most of the remaining exhaust products from the engine. By the time this is accomplished, the portion of the rotor we have been considering has already become an intake chamber of expanding volume again, and a new cycle is under way.

This discussion has so far considered the activities of only one of the three sides of the triangular rotor. The other two sides have in the meantime been performing, in turn, identical functions. Moreover, the engine's other rotor in its own housing, stepped 60 degrees out of phase with the first rotor, has been performing identical functions in the same order.

[A very important quality of the Wankel engine is its ability to put out much more power than a piston engine of comparable size;]or, to put it in another, more significant way, to be much smaller than a piston engine of comparable power. Another quick comparison of the two engines will clarify the reason for the difference, and it is this difference and its enormous potential that has fascinated engineers for decades.

The piston of the four-stroke-cycle engine must make four complete strokes, involving two revolutions of the crankshaft, for every firing of a fuel charge. Thus in a six-cylinder engine, only three firings occur with each revolution of the shaft. In the Wankel, however, three firings for each rotor occur with each rotor revolution, so that in a two-rotor engine like the Mazda, six firings are produced for each revolution of the rotors. Only the firings—not the intake, compression, or exhaust episodes—provide power, and the more firings, the more power.

The simpler structure of the Wankel, with only one-third the number of parts found in a comparable piston engine, also helps make it smaller—and much lighter. Thus the Wankel enjoys both a higher power-to-bulk ratio and a higher power-to-weight ratio, and these qualities contribute to more flexible packaging, including more room under the hood for emissions-control equipment, and a greater overall efficiency.

The piston engine must be provided with two valves per cylinder. The valves must be opened and shut with great accuracy of timing, and this involves a considerable amount of machinery just to perform porting. An expensively machined camshaft must be geared to the crankshaft. Two cams for each cylinder ride against hydraulic or mechanical valve lifters, two for each cylinder, themselves expensive-for-their-size precision assemblies. The lifters ride against push-rods and, in a valve-in-head engine (the most common kind), the push-rods ride against rocker-arms, which in turn push the valves open and allow them to close. The valves themselves must be fitted with powerful springs to snap them shut at the right time. All this machinery is eliminated in the Wankel. Ports (holes) for intake and exhaust, only one for exhaust and two for intake for each rotor, do the job of the valves.

The Wankel is simpler than the piston engine in other ways. Each piston must be connected to a rod via a wrist pin. The rod must be connected to the crankshaft via a journal bearing, which must be amply lubricated. The crankshaft, because of its length, must itself be provided with two to seven main bearings, and these must be amply lubricated. The Wankel has no pistons, wrist pins, or connecting rods, and its main bearings are uncomplicated.

The rotor of the Wankel is geared to a stationary gear mounted on the end housings. Power is transmitted through the rotor to the eccentric shaft directly via the bearing in a method similar to connecting-rod usage.

In the Mazda rotary engine, the rotor housing, the basic component, is an aluminum-alloy casting, and its inner surface has a "waisted" (drawn in at the waist) oval shape called a two-node epitrochoid curve. The rotor housing, together with the end plates or side housings fitted on either side, forms the outer walls of the engine. Spark plugs, two for each rotor housing, are provided; and there are two side-intake ports and a peripheral exhaust port for each rotor housing. The assembly roughly corresponds in function to the cylinders and cylinder head of the piston engine.

The inner surface of the epitrochoidal raceway on the Mazda engine is given a hard chromium surface to increase wear-resistance. (Other manufacturers use different materials.) The

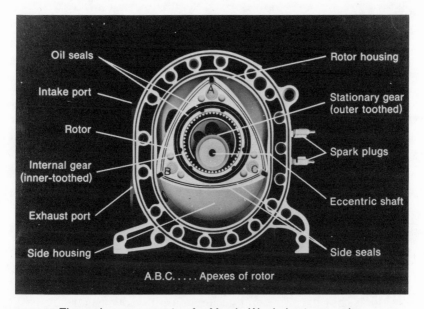

The main components of a Mazda Wankel rotary engine.

housing is honeycombed with passages for the coolant (a standard ethylene glycol mixed with about 50 percent water) to pass through, and there are bolt holes for tension bolts used to clamp the housings together between their side plates.

The rotors of the Mazda engine are made of cast iron, a traditional material for handling changes of temperature with minor distortion. The rotor is roughly triangular but slightly inflated in shape, and because of its odd curves it is called a three-lobe inner envelope of the epitrochoid. The function of piston rings, to seal the piston against the cylinder wall inside which it travels, has already been explained. Sealing of a Wankel rotor—against the epitrochoid raceway and against the end plates covering its sides—is a bit more complicated and indeed was the most serious of the problems besetting the development of the rotary engine. Seals are provided on the rotor to obtain airtightness between the combustion chambers and to prevent lubricating oil from entering the chambers (as in the piston engine: compression rings and oil rings).

On the three peripheral surfaces of each rotor, recesses are provided that become combustion chambers. These are adjustable, as in the cylinder head of a conventional engine, to determine the compression ratio and to give the desired combustion chamber configuration for optimum fuel-burning efficiency.

An internal gear, fixed on one side of the rotor, engages with a stationary gear installed on the side housing to control the movement of the rotor within its housing. In the center section of the rotor a bearing is press-fitted, and into it the eccentric shaft is inserted to support the rotor. The combustion force acting upon the peripheral surface of the rotor is transmitted through the rotor bearing to the eccentric output shaft. With the rotor situated within its housing, three chambers are formed, each enclosed by the inner wall of the housing and one of the three flanks of the rotor.

To enclose the three chambers formed by the rotor and its housing, side housings are clamped to the main housing. But in the case of a two-rotor engine like the Mazda rotary, a housing interposed between the two rotors can serve as the side housing for both rotors because both of its own sides can be utilized. So in a two-rotor engine there are only three side housings—front, intermediate, and rear. In a single-rotor engine, there would be only a front and a rear side housing, like the end frames of an electric motor.

The inner walls of the side housings are finished with flat surfaces so that the sides of the rotors can slide against them. An inlet port is provided on each of these finished side surfaces. Holes provided on the edges of the side housings, identical to those on the main rotor housings, are coolant passages. The side housings are hollow to form a coolant jacket, and a stationary gear is installed in the center of both the front and rear housings.

Each stationary gear engages with an internal gear fixed on the side of the rotor to control its rotation so that the three apexes of the rotor are in constant and even contact with the raceway on the inside of the housing. The ratio of teeth between the stationary gear and the internal gear is 2:3, vital to the operation of this type of rotary engine. The main bearing is inserted into the center section of the rotor.

The crankshaft of the Mazda Wankel corresponds roughly to that of a piston engine except that instead of six or eight rod journals it has two eccentric journals, one for each rotor, that are 180 degrees out of phase. The journals that support the rotors are located in the midsection of the shaft and main journals to support the crankshaft itself are located toward each outer end of the shaft. The rotor journals convert the force obtained from the rotors into torque. The shaft is hollow, containing an oil passage to lubricate the rotor bearings and cool the rotors, which are exposed to combustion temperatures. A small balance weight, gears for the oil pump and distributor, and a V-belt pulley are installed on the front end of the shaft; and on the rear end a flywheel is fitted to even-out the torque and transmit the engine's output to the transmission through

**99**

the clutch; or in the case of an automatic transmission, directly to the transmission via the shaft.

The balance weight, working with the flywheel, balances the centrifugal force acting on the shaft that is caused by the movement of the rotors and the eccentric portions of the shaft.

Needing no valve machinery, the Wankel engine opens and closes its ports by the action of its rotors. An exhaust port is located in the peripheral raceway of each rotor housing. Two inlet ports are provided in the Mazda engine for each working chamber so that the primary stage of the carburetor can be used to supply one inlet port and a secondary stage can supply the second port independently. The diameter of the primary input manifold is small but that of the secondary is large, to meet the requirements of the respective working ranges. The inlet port for the primary stage and that for the secondary face each other in the working chamber of each of the front and rear housings; and therefore a two-stage, four-barrel carburetor is used.

The ignition system used by Mazda appears complicated at first glance, but because the Mazda engine itself is simple, its ignition system is easy to understand. Toyo Kogyo engineers had the advantage, since 1964, of conducting their engine experiments in one of the most sophisticated laboratories in the world. Full computerization was available, and by means of banks of television monitors it was possible to observe twenty-four-hour-a-day simultaneous endurance runs of a number of engines. Every conceivable recording was made on a continuous basis—port timing, rotor temperature, housing temperatures at various points, fuel mixture, and many other engine functions including, of course, spark timing.

After about three years of intensive investigation it was decided to use two spark plugs for each rotor in order to promote the most complete combustion possible. This decision was not made lightly, because it meant doubling the whole ignition system of the engine—two distributors, two ignition coils, and two sets of primary and secondary wires and cables,

**100**

one each for the leading and trailing spark plug. (Since there are two rotors, there are four spark plugs. The two leading plugs, one for each rotor, are supplied by one of the ignition systems, and the two trailing plugs are supplied by the other system, which is identical except in the matter of timing.)

[In any comparison of the piston engine with the rotary, it must be kept in mind that while in the piston engine the combustion chamber stands still and the piston moves up and down toward it and away from it, in the rotary the combustion chambers are constantly on the move as they are created by the circular-combined-with-eccentric motion of the rotor. When the intake port is uncovered and induction of the fuel mixture begins, the mixture flows into the newly created combustion chamber at a rather high speed and *in the same direction as the rotor is moving*. This makes for great turbulence in the fuel charge, an advantage in combustion. By the time the combustion chamber has moved around to the vicinity of the spark plugs and is at full compression and ready for firing, it is extremely long and narrow, whereas at top dead center in the piston engine the chamber is more or less biscuit-shaped. The rotary's chamber has an enormous amount of surface area for its volume, allowing good heat transfer to the cooling jacket and keeping combustion temperatures lower than are found in the piston engine. This is thought to be the chief reason for the rotary's low production of oxides of nitrogen (NOx). This makes exhaust clean-up simpler, easier, and consequently cheaper in the rotary as compared with the problem in the piston engine.]

In the many Toyo Kogyo experiments involved in the development of the Mazda engine, various configurations of the rotor-housing raceway were tested. Many types of seals had to be tried in the finally successful effort to discover materials and designs that would provide acceptable engine endurance and longevity. In about three years more than five thousand rotor housings were run to destruction and discarded. This massive cut-and-try procedure was possible, even for a company as

**101**

large and prosperous as Toyo Kogyo, only because the Mazda engineers had at their disposal Toyo Kogyo's own machine-tool division, which could supply a steady stream of precisely machined housings for the experimental work.

The outline of the epitrochoidal raceway has the appearance of an oval that is pinched in at the waist. The Japanese call it a "waisted oval." The pinched-in point, being the narrowest measurement, is called the minor axis, and it is at this point on the engine's left side (or the right side if you're looking at the front of the engine, the aspect of most illustrations) that top dead center is reached and ignition occurs.

Two spark plugs are provided, one just above and one just below the minor axis, and they are called "trailing" and "leading," respectively. The leading plug always fires first and an instant later is "backed up" by the trailing plug, not only to insure combustion but to provide more complete combustion than would occur if only one plug were used.

Each of the two housings of the Mazda rotary engine is cast with a number of channels that form a water jacket around each combustion chamber to manage excess heat, in much the same manner employed in conventional liquid-cooled engines. The coolant delivered by the water pump first arrives at the front housing and moves through some of the passages on the outer edges of the front, first rotor, intermediate, second rotor, and rear housing. Here the coolant turns, crosses the rear housing and turns again to move forward through the cooler side of the engine—rear rotor housing, intermediate, front rotor, and back to the front housing. The coolant thus distributes heat from the warm side of the engine to the cooler side to maintain the even temperature needed to prevent warping and other aberrations that would interfere with smooth engine operation.

Hot coolant is then sent to the radiator to be reduced in temperature before being recirculated to the engine, as in conventional engines. An interesting temperature regulation method, using (in engines produced since August, 1968) a

**102**

bottom-bypass type thermostat, will be discussed in Chapter 9.

The parts of the rotary engine that are subjected to the highest temperatures are the rotors. Since it so far has not proved practical to attempt to cool the rapidly spinning members from a supply of coolant from the engine's regular cooling system, the rotors are instead cooled by a constant delivery of oil through the hollow crankshaft.

Lubrication of the engine is fairly conventional, with oil being picked up from the bottom of the pan and delivered via pump pressure to the various bearings and gas seals. The bearings are force-fed from a trochoidal pump. One departure, however, is the necessary use of an oil cooler, similar to a small radiator, because of the high rotor temperatures. Oil from the engine drops to the pan, is picked up and sent through the pump to the cooler, then to the oil filter, then directly to the main bearings.

Another departure involves protection of the apex seals, which otherwise would not receive adequate cooling, lubrication, and assistance in their gas-sealing job at the combustion chambers. A portion of the engine oil leaving the filter is tapped, and through a special metering oil pump is delivered to the carburetor to be mixed with the fuel. The amount of oil thus consumed is governed by speed and load of the engine and is extremely small, in the neighborhood of a quart in 1,500 miles of highway driving.

The Mazda rotary engine is easier to service than any comparable piston engine on the market. It can be "pulled" from the car in an hour and completely "torn down" in about two hours on the bench. A major overhaul could be accomplished in about 35 percent less time than required for similar work on a comparable piston engine. Certain parts are expensive, but this could change with increased mass production. At the present time a major overhaul costs somewhat less than on a conventional piston engine of comparable horsepower, and rotary overhaul costs will undoubtedly go even lower.

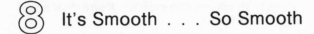

# 8 It's Smooth . . . So Smooth

The field of automotive engineering dominated the technological development of the United States during the entire first half of the twentieth century. Yet with all the millions of man-hours devoted to the sciences and crafts

104

involved in automobile production, another endeavor concurrently received an even larger investment of human time—the art of driving.

Driving an early automobile was easy and fun, but not in the sense we would apply those words to driving today. For the old-timers it was an adventure. Getting an engine started was a victory in itself; putting the car into motion and steering it on a course that avoided collision was a courageous undertaking generally ˙applauded by bystanders. For many people, just committing oneself to being a passenger took a certain amount of resolution, and it was an experience long talked about afterwards.

The early car was easy to drive because there was plenty of room—you could park wherever you stopped the car or it stopped you, and there were few other automobiles to evade. After a few minutes of instruction, a novice could take the wheel and steer his vehicle all around the town—if nothing got in his way. When brakes and lights were added, drivers felt that automobiles were at last truly safe to operate.

Right from the outset women became involved in the reckless sport of motoring, and but for one shortcoming—comparative physical weakness—would have become as avid in their enthusiasm for the new gas buggies as their husbands and brothers were.

Hand-cranking an engine was difficult for women and risky for anyone who didn't perform the task expertly. If, due to improper spark advance, a plug should fire while a piston was still traveling upward on its compression stroke, the engine would be spun rapidly backward, jerking the crank out of the user's hand and flipping it around to strike him on the wrist. Many thousands of broken arms resulted from car-cranking mishaps.

But the self-starter put the woman firmly and literally in the driver's seat, where she promptly found herself described by the uncomplimentary term "woman driver." If there was any justification for this attitude that implied that women were

**105**

inept drivers, their problems undoubtedly stemmed from the clutch, transmission, and steering mechanisms. Early clutches were extremely stiff, requiring strength and weight to operate them. Transmissions were not synchronized and, particularly in cold weather when the heavy oil in the gearbox tended to solidify, next to impossible for a woman to shift with one hand.

But of the three problems, a stiff steering system was the most continuously demanding of strength, and the difficulty of maneuvering into parking spaces and in tight traffic situations often caused trouble for all but the most robust women. However, in the normal course of development, and as tires became wider in tread and softer, particularly in the 1930s and 1940s, much attention was given to steering-gear ratios and refinement of methods of turning the front wheels with the least possible amount of effort on the part of the driver.

Oddly, as time went on, the largest and heaviest cars, mounting increasingly heavier engines and accessories such as radiators at their front ends, became easier to steer than the smaller cars, on which for reasons of economy little money was spent in steering-system design and application. Then, at just about the time when steering had evolved to the point where most drivers could handle the wheel with little effort, power steering was introduced, in 1951, on Chrysler and Buick products. This was the same year in which the one-hundred-millionth American passenger car was assembled.

Within a decade, women's increasing use of the family car, the fact that more than 20 percent of all car-owning families had two or more cars, and the rapid rise in single women who owned cars finally increased the number of women drivers to more than 44 percent of the entire driving population of the United States. Even considering that many men's sole occupation is driving (truckers, salesmen, cab drivers, chauffeurs, etc.) and that many men must drive in conjunction with their work, for the last several years there have been almost as many female as male drivers in the United States. Of course this was only partly due to the availability of self-starters, automatic transmissions, and power steering, but these three conveniences certainly promoted the distaff-driver boom in this country.

On small cars power steering never was necessary or even important—the forces needed to turn the front wheels of a vehicle under 2,500 pounds in curb weight are indeed small. Automatic transmission is only a luxury convenience in any car, never a necessity—except for the driver who has not learned to use a clutch. There are today many hundreds of thousands of young men and women who cannot drive a car that is not equipped with an automatic transmission.

The clutch does two things: it provides an interruptible connection between the engine and the wheels so the engine can idle when the car is stopped and gears can be changed while the car is moving, and it provides a sliding contact through which the connection is made. When shifting manually, the driver decides upon the engine or wheel speeds at which gear changes are made; with an automatic transmission such decisions are made only partly by the driver and partly by a governor in the transmission itself. For this reason, race drivers, who must shift at varying speeds depending on the circumstances, almost universally employ a manual transmission, which does no thinking for them.

When the driver "lets out" the clutch, the driving plate, which is connected to the engine and is in motion, is allowed to bear on the driven plate, which is connected to the power (usually rear) wheels. This causes the driven plate to begin to move and pick up speed as the pressure increases while the clutch pedal rises from the floor. But because energy to move the car must be increased by the engine, it is necessary to depress the accelerator gradually while the clutch is being engaged gradually. Of all the things the neophyte driver must learn, this two-footed coordinated action is perhaps the most difficult. The automatic transmission, which handles the clutch

**107**

action internally through turbine-like wheels running close to each other in an oil bath, eliminates all but the acceleration action from this part of the driver's duties.

The driver with an automatic transmission can control to some extent the engine-and-wheel speeds at which the gears change—speeds are higher if the accelerator pedal is depressed more. In the Mazda, the only car with a rotary engine that can be purchased by American buyers during most of 1974, there is a considerable difference between the effect on the driver of a car with automatic transmission and a car with the four-speed stick-shift. It is important that the difference be discussed, since in the upcoming General Motors rotary-equipped car, the Vega, approximately the same differences in acceleration, engine speeds at which gear changes are made, and driver's control over the vehicle can be expected.

The Mazda with automatic transmission and the Mazda without such power assistance are actually two different automobiles, so far as the driver and his "feel" for the car are concerned. The main difference lies in the fact that the Mazda rotary engine typically develops its really powerful and interesting torque at a speed higher than usual in many piston engines.

In manual shifting on any car, the driver can let his accelerator foot lead his clutch foot, with the result of a higher engine speed at engagement. And if he wishes he can depress the accelerator after engagement and hold it depressed for an extra moment, so that acceleration is rapid and engine (and car) speeds are higher at the time of shifting to second gear. For continuing rapid acceleration in second and subsequent gears, the same technique can be followed. What actually happens is that as the driver becomes accustomed to the engine-transmission mix in his particular car, he can accelerate slowly or rapidly as he pleases and as traffic conditions allow or dictate. The race driver, to whom acceleration is all-important, naturally uses a technique much different from one acceptable in ordinary traffic. And nonprofessional drivers must operate their vehicles according to the need of the moment but within the confines of the traffic regulations.

The driver who has the use of an automatic transmission can do the same. But his engine-speed choices are limited to the setting of a governor inside the transmission and to the two or three gear ratios provided in most types of automatic transmissions. If he wants a fast getaway he merely depresses the accelerator pedal farther; this causes his engine to reach a higher speed before each gear change occurs. For ordinary driving this is sufficient—the driver can make a fast getaway when he chooses, or he can drive sedately whenever he wishes. When testing of cars is performed by skillful drivers, however, higher acceleration rates can almost always be achieved by those who use manual transmissions, thus the preference for them by race drivers.

As late as mid-1974 the only brand of rotary-engine car available for demonstration to the public was the Mazda. This, however, was no problem because the Mazda line covered the most common types of automobiles expected to mount rotary engines for the next several years: neither pure sports cars nor sedate passenger sedans but rather a group of sporty little two-door and four-door configurations, an RX-4 station wagon introduced in January, and a "sport" compact pickup truck that was introduced in the United States in March as the world's first rotary-powered truck. (Mazda has long built a line of piston-powered cars and trucks.)

In driving a small piston-engine, manual-transmission car, the driver usually leaves it in first gear until the engine is up to about 3,000 rpm, then shifts into second until the engine again gets up to 3,000 rpm or slightly higher, then goes to third for cruising around town. Usually, fourth speed is reserved for freeway and highway speeds above 30 mph because fourth gear in most small cars has very little pickup power. Speeds lower than 30 mph in this gear can cause the engine to "lug," with possible damage to bearings, rods, and the crankshaft. Lugging happens when the fuel charges are burned too infrequently so

**109**

that the engine puts out its power in widely-spaced surges instead of the normal flow of crankshaft torque that occurs when the engine is running at a proper speed.

Each gear in the transmission provides a maximum speed beyond which engine damage can occur from overrunning, and a minimum speed below which the engine should not be operated. Every driver soon familiarizes himself with his vehicle in these important respects. With an automatic transmission, the driver merely accelerates according to how fast he wants his vehicle to reach cruising speed—for city traffic or for the highway—and the gearbox does the shifting for him.

In the Mazda rotary with manual transmission, selection of speeds for each gear is much less critical because of two interesting ways in which the rotary differs from the piston engine: It is capable of much higher rotational speeds without potential damage to internal parts; and it does not "lug" in the conventional sense because it does not have to utilize the stop-start action of pistons.

Thus with the Mazda rotary the driver can, if he wishes, pull away from the curb in first and accelerate his engine to as high as 7,000 rpm, then shift directly into fourth. Or he can use all his gears, in order, just as if he were driving a conventional car. Once in fourth, which he can use in slow city driving down to 25 mph or even slower, he doesn't have to worry about lugging his engine even if he slows his car to the point of engine-idle speed. This gives the driver a great deal of flexibility: he can shift up or down as he wishes for better control in tight traffic situations, or he can cruise around town with little or no thought to shifting as long as his car keeps moving. At a nominal 2,000 rpm of engine speed, the car travels about 8 mph in first gear, about 15 mph in second, about 25 mph in third, and about 34 mph in fourth gear. This engine speed of 2,000 rpm is considerably above the 750-rpm idle speed of an automatic-transmission rotary standing in "drive" or the 900-rpm idle of a manual-transmission rotary. Ordinary piston-engine idle speed is in the 500-600-rpm range.

The automatic transmission available on both the RX-2 and the later-model RX-3, while more convenient for more drivers, curtails some of the engine-speed choices because the transmission will automatically shift when the engine speed reaches a certain point, depending on how far the accelerator pedal is depressed, as explained earlier. For a normal takeoff from zero mph, shifting will occur at about 4,000 rpm.

All Mazda rotary models have in common the quality of not disappointing drivers used to larger cars and of surprising small-car drivers by providing a big-car road-handling effect. The author's first experience with a Mazda was in Oklahoma with a brand-new car provided by Mazda of Tulsa, an RX-2 with stick-shift. During many hours of test-driving, the little car convinced the author, ordinarily a standard-to-big car driver, that this small car was different.

The car was taken on back roads, some of them in various states of disrepair, and on the Will Rogers Turnpike. Driving around the city also provided an opportunity to test the car against railroad tracks, chuckholes, and the usual bad driving features found in a big city. Moving from a big car to a Mazda was not the traumatic experience that was anticipated.

The next Mazda the author tested was one purchased by his daughter at his suggestion, an RX-3 with stick-shift. It too displayed the big-car riding qualities found in the RX-2 and, being equipped with air conditioning and an excellent AM-FM radio, was in every sense a luxury small car. It has performed faultlessly, has had no service other than warranty check-ins, and at 5,000 miles in 1974, seems to be in top running condition.

Finally, the author put about 600 miles on a demonstrator that already had 1,000 miles on the odometer. This was an RX-2 with automatic transmission, and one aspect of the rotary engine that could be considered disadvantageous showed up. The rotary engine differs from the piston engine in one noticeable respect: whereas the piston engine develops its torque at a rather low crankshaft speed and has almost instantaneous response to the accelerator pedal, the rotary

**111**

develops its torque at a somewhat higher speed. The difference may be only a matter of 1,000 rpm or less—nothing to think about in a stick-shift model, where the driver can decide for himself the speed at which to change gears; but in the automatic-transmission Mazda it seemed that gear changes came too soon. This gave the effect of sluggishness, especially at lower speeds when the engine did not have the opportunity to develop powerful torque. Although the author was assured by factory representatives that this was an adjustable matter, it seemed that full advantage was not being taken of the engine's capability—so obvious on stick-shift models—to perform well at higher rotational speeds.

This is not to say that the engine misfired or otherwise acted up at lower speeds. As a matter of fact, with all the early years of talk about the difficulty with idle and low-speed performance, much attention was given that controversial area, and the Mazdas driven by the author performed faultlessly. The noticeable slowness of acceleration at the low-speed end under automatic-transmission selection of gear-change was, however, in contrast to performance of models with manuals that the author was able to shift for himself.

Mazda's gasoline mileage could stand some improvement. Highway mileage of 22 mpg with stick-shift and without air conditioning is not good for a car with a curb weight of less than 2,200 pounds, an RX-3 two-door. The slightly larger RX-2, with air conditioning and an automatic transmission, showed only 16.5 mpg in 70-mph interstate-highway driving. Piston-engine cars of comparable weight can be expected to get several more miles per gallon. Understand that only nonprofessional (that is, not economy-run) driving is being considered here. With just a bit more development time, it's a certainty that Toyo Kogyo engineers will be able to improve their gas-mileage readings. Meanwhile, the piston-engine readings continue to deteriorate as more and more pollution controls are added, and Mazda, already able to comply with original 1976 emission

112

specifications, is expected to look better by comparison during the next couple of years.

Two aspects of Mazda rotary-driving cannot be overemphasized. The first is an incredible smoothness and quiet, especially at highway speeds, compared to any small piston-engine car on today's market. The quality is so prominent that, as the driver begins to get used to the absence of engine noise and vibration, he becomes irritated by sounds generally ignored in a comparable-size piston-engine car, such as tire-tread singing and the rush of air around the body. The same quality can of course be expected in any future rotary-engine car that equals Mazda's highway driveability.

The second extraordinary feature of the Mazda—and it, too, will hopefully be incorporated in all upcoming rotaries regardless of brand—is a magnificent passing ability at highway speeds. In the majority of small cars, discounting muscle-cars, lack of pickup is one of the most distressing and dangerous disadvantages. But the Mazda rotary, with its excellent power-to-weight ratio combined with a high torque curve, displays excellent acceleration at the faster end of its cruising-speed range.

Overall, the Mazda with a rotary engine is more than a satisfactory car—it's an exciting little car that has great appeal for the modern American driver, as indicated by its recent sales record. Moreover, in sharp contrast to the competitors in its size- and price-range, it can hug the road at 100 mph and show a capability of traveling at even higher speeds for prolonged periods of time. This is not legal on our highways, of course, but it is demonstrative of the heavy-duty ability of an engine that has built public confidence in the United States in only three years.

Get in an ordinary piston-engine car and wind it up to 7,000 rpm as you go from one gear to another and you will probably damage its powerplant. The fact that a rotary engine is not damaged by such treatment is important in more ways than one. An engine that can survive sustained high rotational speeds is an engine that is well balanced, does not contain inherent vibration factors of considerable potential, and has good built-in longevity. The Mazda rotary engine qualifies on these points and has the additional capability of gaining power at higher speeds, a quality not shared by its competitors in the piston category.

If it does nothing else, the rotary engine will appeal to Americans who have been looking for something new and exciting. But the rotary offers a bonus: the ability to provide transportation with next to zero pollution, and it is on this score that the rotary bids fair to becoming the engine of our immediate future.

# 9 Take Care of Me, Or I Quit

In any consideration of the mechanical aspects of the rotary engine there are those features that it shares with the conventional piston engine and those that are peculiar to it alone. There are sharp contrasts: The rotary can stand the abuse of a high rotational speed that would shortly cause a piston engine to fly to pieces; a rotary must receive regular attention to its oil-pan supply of motor oil because it is *supposed* to burn oil while most standard-production piston engines burn oil only when they are defective in some serious way.

For the sake of brevity, some of the design characteristics that are shared by the two kinds of engines (mainly in their accessories) will be passed over quickly while emphasis will be placed on the areas where the rotary differs markedly from the piston engine. For practical purposes, discussion of the Wankel rotary will center around the Mazda brand because it is the only one available in quantity to the American consumer. When the General Motors RC comes to the market in substantial numbers, any differences in theory and practice between it and the Mazda from the standpoint of maintenance will be adequately handled by the owner's manual.

With the piston engine until recent years the generally accepted practice, with the blessing of the engineers, was to crank it until it started, then go. This recommendation was modified when emission-controlled engines produced since 1968 were discovered to be finicky during warm-up. Accordingly, it was announced that when a cold engine was started it should be adequately warmed up so that when the car was brought into traffic the engine would perform dependably and not buck and stagger when accelerated.

For an entirely different reason, the same advice is given to the owner of a rotary engine. It is important that the internal components of a rotary be gradually warmed up to a uniform running temperature to avoid undue thermal stress. This prevents the possibility of warping and consequent poor gas-sealing when the engine is put under load.

With an automatic transmission the shift selector must be placed in either the "neutral" or "park" positions, the only positions that will allow the starting circuit to function. With a manual transmission the owner is advised first to depress the

**116**

clutch pedal and shift to the "neutral" position; this disconnects the engine from the transmission so the starter motor does not have to turn transmission gears in their heavy-oil bath.

For the first start of the day at atmospheric temperatures under 90 degrees F., the manual choke is always used to obtain a quick and pollution-free start. With the choke knob pulled and without his foot on the accelerator, the driver turns the ignition key to "start" position to crank the engine.

A special technique is employed for a start in below-zero weather. Before beginning the above procedure, the driver presses a special "Starting Assist" button that supplies a "starting fluid" (90 percent ethylene glycol permanent anti-freeze and 10 percent water) to the air-gasoline fuel charge to be burned in the combustion chambers. It is emphasized that the "Starting Assist" button is used only for severe cold-weather starting and never when the engine is warm. The glycol fluid is not compatible with engine oil, and excessive use of it will not only contaminate the oil but also could lead to spark plug fouling and future starting difficulties. In a severe climate where the fluid must be used often, the engine oil should be changed more often than at the recommended 4,000-mile intervals.

After the engine is started, the clutch pedal (with transmission in neutral) should be let out and the choke control knob depressed to the half-way position. Since the choke lever is connected to the accelerator linkage, this will keep the engine at "fast idle" of about 1,800 rpm. It is recommended that a cold engine be thus warmed up for about three minutes (two minutes with automatic transmission), and then the choke should be pressed in all the way. Excessive choking, as with other types of engines, feeds a rich mixture to the engine and will cause spark plug fouling if prolonged.

You do not use the choke—which is strictly a cold-starting aid—in extremely hot weather or if the engine is still warm from previous running. Instead, a slightly different starting technique is employed: Without pumping the accelerator pedal, depress it approximately half way. Holding the pedal in that position, crank the engine; and immediately when it starts, release the key and the accelerator pedal.

An emergency low-battery start can be performed on a car equipped with manual transmission by pushing or towing. In addition to the extraordinary care that must be taken with any kind of car in such a situation, there are two important things to remember during a push- or tow-start of the Mazda: Only third gear should be used, and clutch engagement should take place only at 10 to 12 mph. Less than that speed will not adequately crank the engine; a higher speed will put an undue strain on the entire power train from wheels to engine.

The Mazda is equipped with a standard speedometer-odometer combination for indication of speed and mileage, both accumulated and trip. It is additionally equipped with an electric tachometer for indication of engine revolutions-per-minute. The dial is yellow-lined from 6,000 to 7,000 rpm and red-lined at 7,000 rpm. Since the engine can easily be "revved up" far beyond the red line, the owner is cautioned never to let this happen, since severe engine damage could result. As a nominal guide while the new owner is getting used to the unusual engine, the factory suggests that speeds in the various gears be kept within the following ranges:

First gear, 0–25 mph; Second gear, 12–40 mph; Third gear, 20–60 mph; Fourth gear, above 25 mph. As you see, considerable latitude of speeds in each gear can be allowed with a rotary engine. It will not "lug" at low speeds; but on the other hand it performs best, the factory advises, at speeds above 1,500 rpm and all the way up to 5,500; thus its excellent passing ability on the highway, a quality rarely found in small cars.

The rotary engine does not detonate, or "knock." Anti-knock-quality gasoline is therefore not only unnecessary but should not be used except in an emergency. The preferred fuel is no-lead or low-lead gasoline. Since no-lead gas is not universally available, the driver has the happy option of purchasing the lowest-price gasoline he can find, since this will usually mean lowest-lead content, on which the Mazda will thrive. Eventually, extremely low-octane gasoline may be put on the market to supply the rapidly growing number of rotaries on the road. The Mazda can use fuel with an octane rating as low as 70—not even on the market yet—and when low-octane gasoline does become available it should be the cheapest fuel on the market, since it requires minimum refining and no additive of expensive tetraethyl lead.

The new rotary engine should be given a minimum break-in period of about 600 miles. During this time the driver should try to avoid sudden stops and fast starts, should not race the engine in neutral, and should avoid heavy acceleration and high engine speeds on the highway, keeping the tachometer at varying speeds under 3,000 rpm. At 600 miles (2,000 miles on 1974 models) the car should be returned to the dealership for its first checkup, which will include an all-important change of oil. Thereafter, oil changes need be made only at 4,000-mile intervals, unless extremely heavy-duty driving is involved. This includes a large amount of low-speed, around-the-town driving in short trips under five miles each; a lot of extremely high-speed driving; driving in very dusty conditions; or abusive driving such as "dragging" or other abnormal uses of the engine. For heavy-duty driving it is advisable to change engine oil at 2,000-mile intervals or even oftener.

The manufacturer recommends that the oil level be checked at every fuel stop, to be on the safe side. The engine is provided with a special metering oil pump (not found on piston-type engines) that supplies a miniscule amount of lubricating oil directly from the oil filter to the carburetor, to be mixed and burned with the fuel. This tiny oil supply is for the purpose of lubricating the apex and corner seals (at each point of each rotor) and helping them with their sealing job. A normal Mazda engine thus consumes oil for this purpose at the rate of about one quart every 1,500 miles. At 60 mph this would convert to every twenty-five hours, but the amount varies with speed and load to provide optimum lubrication protection. Also, an

**119**

aberration in the metering device could cause abnormally high or low consumption, either of which would shortly result in erratic engine performance. Thus a special caution to the rotary-engine owner: Check the oil level frequently for possible malfunction of this unique engine lubricating system.

Proper function of the metering oil pump system is checked by your mechanic as follows: Disconnect the two oil tubes from the metering pump at the carburetor. Set engine idle temporarily at 2,000 rpm. Run engine for a minute or so until output of oil from tubes is steady. Then start catching the oil in a metric-measured cup. Take oil for exactly ten minutes, then stop engine. Measure oil taken—it should be in the amount of 4.5 cubic centimeters, plus or minus 1 cc. If outside the 1-cc. tolerance, the amount should be adjusted by turning the special adjusting screw one turn—clockwise to increase flow and counterclockwise to decrease. The test should then be repeated and any further adjustment made to get the flow within tolerance. If adjustment cannot be made satisfactorily, the entire metering pump assembly should be replaced, as it performs a vital function in the Mazda rotary engine.

In small cars, an air conditioning system imposes a severe load on the engine at idle and slow speeds. The Mazda handles that problem with a "throttle" knob on the dash (actually a cable connected to the accelerator linkage), which when pulled raises the idle speed of the engine enough to provide effective cooling in traffic without the possibility of stalling.

The air-pollution-control systems in the Mazda are three: an engine ventilation system, an evaporative emission control system, and an exhaust emission control system. The engine ventilation system corresponds to the PCV system in piston engines. Blowby gases in the engine housing are drawn into the intake manifold to be burned with the carbureted intake mixture. There is a valve similar to the PCV valve to control the flow, and fresh air is inducted into the engine housing from the air cleaner.

The evaporative emission control setup is designed to pre-

120

vent escape of gasoline vapor into the open air from the fuel system. Vapor rising from the surface of the gasoline in the fuel tank is channeled into a condensing tank and later fed back into the fuel tank when the engine is not running. Fuel vapor that has not condensed in the special tank is pulled into an air space of the engine and trapped in a charcoal filter there. Vapor that develops in the fuel tank when the engine is running is pulled directly through the ventilation valve to the intake manifold to be burned in the combustion chambers. When the engine is running, fuel trapped in the charcoal filter is vaporized by fresh air from the air cleaner and is pulled through the ventilation valve, mixed with fresh air and blowby gases, and burned in the engine.

The exhaust emission control system consists of an air injection arrangement, ignition and air-flow adjustments, and a deceleration control system that are not unlike those found in conventional late-model cars. But in addition, the Mazda has a thermal reactor on 1970, 1971, 1972, 1973, and 1974 rotary engine models, which, combined with the other pollution-control systems, made it possible for Mazda to pass the federal emission specifications for the years 1975 and 1976.

The thermal reactor is a muffler-like device that is bolted directly on the engine in place of an exhaust manifold so that the exhaust gases entering it are still quite hot and still combusting. As the gases are directed into the chamber of the thermal reactor they are shot with outside air by means of a belt-driven air pump. The oxygen in the fresh air, combining with the combusting gases, furthers the combustion process through oxidizing that successfully renders the unburned hydrocarbons and carbon monoxide into harmless water vapor and carbon dioxide. Offensive products are reduced to levels below the maximums allowed by the federal standards.

The thermal reactor is subjected to extremes of temperature, and the first discernible defect in it would likely be a crack in its metal jacket. However, except for possible factory defects in materials and workmanship, which are warranted for 50,000

**121**

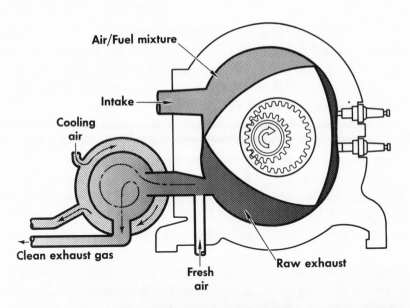

Air/Fuel mixture

Intake

Cooling air

Clean exhaust gas

Fresh air

Raw exhaust

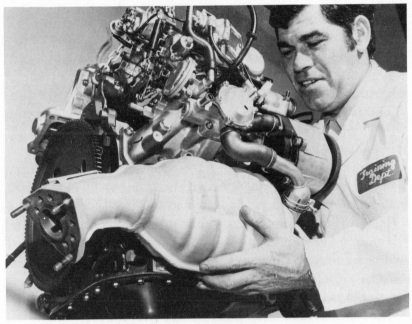

A simplified drawing of the Mazda Wankel rotary engine equipped with a thermal reactor for emissions control.
At the technician's left hand is the thermal reactor, the chief component in the Mazda engine's emissions-control system.

122

miles or five years in newly purchased cars, it is not likely for such cracks to show up until the thermal reactor is old and worn out (the factory estimates it will last for at least 150,000 miles), and repairs should not be considered—the thermal reactor should be replaced.

The water-antifreeze coolant, the fuel filter, the oil filter, and the engine oil are changed at the same intervals as on conventional automobiles, with the same cautions for heavy-duty or dusty conditions that call for more frequent service. The air cleaner element is a cleanable type, however, that should be cleaned every 4,000 miles. Under dusty conditions, the intervals are halved.

The four spark plugs in the Mazda rotary are specially designed for rotary use. They should be checked *every 4,000 miles*, and if found damaged or too fouled to clean, they should be replaced. Because they are special, they must be replaced with identical factory equipment or plugs approved by your dealer's service manager, to avoid warranty violation and possible engine damage.

Ignition timing on a rotary engine is an extremely critical adjustment. It is carried out in the same way as on conventional piston engines, however, except that there are two timing marks (one for the leading and one for the trailing spark system) on the eccentric-shaft pulley. Timing of each system is done separately but in the usual way, with strobe timing light connected to either a leading or a trailing plug, the distributor vacuum hose disconnected and the hose plugged, and the engine idle set at 900 rpm.

Starting-assist fluid, a mixture of 90 percent ethylene glycol (permanent antifreeze) and 10 percent water, is carried in a reservoir located just above the steering gearbox. After refilling, the function of the system should be checked by removing the air-cleaner housing and observing the fluid spurting into the carburetor throat when the "Start Assist" button is pushed.

The cooling system of the Mazda rotary is fairly conventional (with water pump, thermostat, radiator, cooling jacket, associated hoses for radiator and hot-water heater) and differs from the cooling system of a piston engine in only a few respects. Temperature regulation is by means of a wax-type thermostat having a bottom by-pass valve that works against a by-pass hole leading to the engine. Note that the thermostat is not a straight in-line type as found on many automobiles. On the Mazda bottom by-pass installation the by-pass hole is much larger than found on the in-line type. When the thermostat is fully closed, a large amount of coolant is allowed to circulate to prevent any local rise in the coolant temperature. When operating temperature is reached and the thermostat is fully opened, the thermostat valve closes the by-pass hole to the engine, and all of the coolant flows through the radiator for maximum cooling. If, however, the thermostat were removed, the large by-pass hole leading the coolant back to the engine would detract from the circulation through the radiator, and the coolant temperature would rise to the point of engine damage. The thermostat, therefore, should never be removed from the system, and no other type of thermostat should be substituted.

For the most satisfactory performance to be expected from a rotary engine of the Mazda type, the driver need remember only these six essential points:

1. Warm up the engine gradually and sufficiently before shifting into gear. Should horsepower output be suddenly increased in a still-cold engine, the engine's internal temperatures will be locally increased too quickly while coolant temperature is still low. This can result in the development of undue thermal stress in certain areas with the possibility of damage to component parts. Proper warmup means gradually spreading an increasing temperature throughout the entire engine, with a minimum of local "hot spots."

2. Do not overspeed the engine. A driver used to the noise and vibrations of a piston engine can inadvertently run a quiet and smooth rotary engine past the red line on the tachometer. This will shorten the life of the engine. The driver of a new

124

rotary should pay special attention to his gear changes, with a wary eye on the tachometer dial.

3. Never race the engine. A rotary, like other types of engines, is designed to operate under various amounts of load. A completely no-load situation, as in "gunning" the engine in neutral, makes for poor sealing and an unrestricted looseness of internal components that will result in premature aging of the engine.

4. Don't experiment with the spark timing. If the engine is operated with ignition advance that is not within factory specifications, poor performance and possible engine damage will result.

5. Never install substitute spark plugs. The specially designed factory-installed plugs must be replaced with authorized parts.

6. Check the engine oil frequently to make sure the engine *is consuming* the proper amount.

The rotary engine is different—like nothing else you've driven. Most mechanics still don't know the first thing about its maintenance and repair. Therefore, the rotary owner will be well advised to read and comply with the instructions in his owner's manual, carefully guard his engine and drive-train warranty, and let his dealer provide all needed services. The dealers and their service managers may not yet know all the answers regarding rotary repair. But authorized factory know-how is readily available to them through company field representatives, so let them take the responsibility.

# 10 From Felix to the Future

Never before in the long history of the automobile has a technological development received as much attention in the press as the Wankel engine. Early cautious words back in the 1950s dealt mainly with its "new," "unusual," or "unique" aspects, with little information concerning its actual possibilities as an automotive powerplant. In the early 1960s, after engines had been run publicly, there was some speculation that the Wankel might eventually be used in automobiles—but only after many years, perhaps decades, of further development. The positive strides made by NSU and the Wankel company received only minimum press coverage, while announcements from Curtiss-Wright were mainly reflected in the financial pages.

Toyo Kogyo was virtually unheard of in the United States until after the first few rotary-engine cars were shipped to the West Coast in 1970. Now there was something to talk about—the little cars could be seen, driven, and bought. News of them exploded across the continent, and before the next year was ended nearly every automotive writer in the country had had something to say about the Mazda.

Almost without exception, Mazda received good press. The metropolitan newspapers featured in-depth articles explaining the Wankel engine, and the car-buff magazines went wild with testing, retesting, and evaluating—often reporting in slightly amazed tones when they discovered that the innovative engines neither blew up nor fell apart.

In mid-1972, *Changing Times*, the family economics magazine of the Kiplinger Washington Editors, Inc., asked the popular question in an article (written by the author) titled: "Is the Wankel the Auto Engine of the Future?" GM had invested a down payment of $5 million and had made a second payment of $10 million; it began to look as if GM was getting serious about the Wankel.

In other media, speculation picked up rapidly: Did GM know something no one else knew—was the Wankel going to take over completely from the piston engine? At first, GM officials had cautiously optimistic words for their rotary-engine investigation project—things were going smoothly, and "soon" there would be some definite word. This led to unfounded forecasts in the press that made it appear that every major car maker in the world was on the verge of some big deal that would lead to manufacture of his own version of the Wankel. The Wankel wrangle appeared to be getting out of hand.

GM then adopted a closed-mouth attitude on the Wankel, at least in its engineering and public relations departments, and only top officials such as the board chairman and the president would speak to the press in any detail. In early August, 1973, at a University of Michigan seminar, the GM president, Edward N. Cole, announced that his company would produce 100,000 Wankel-powered Vegas "starting in 1974."

Cole's son, Dr. David Cole, an associate professor at the University of Michigan's department of mechanical engineering, is a respected engineer who enjoys the privilege of speaking his personal opinions without having his words attributed to GM, in spite of the fact that his father is president of the company. Dr. Cole has long expressed optimism regarding the Wankel (which he, like the GM people, always calls the "rotary") but he employs plenty of professional conservativeness in his statements.

At the university's Second Automotive Emissions Conference, as reported in the September 24, 1973 *Automotive News*, he said, "We must look at the rotary engine with caution, but it is a source of change. We must look beyond the engine and at its total application. The major car field for the rotary engine is in the mid-size class of cars." He added, however, that he felt that larger cars would provide a less expensive application for the rotary of the future on a cost per car-pound basis. He ventured that the rotary engine might eventually cut the weight of some cars by as much as a thousand pounds. But he was most enthusiastic about the compactness of the rotary and its ability to decrease an auto-front-end length. "I view the front space of a car as a liability," he stated.

With the understatement, "The rotary engine is a highly transient art at this time," Dr. Cole said that even though engine pollution has been a highly publicized topic, other factors such as engine size and cost are actually more impor-

A view of the left side of a General Motors prototype 200 cubic inch Wankel rotary engine.

Board chairman Richard C. Gerstenberg (left) and president Edward N. Cole of General Motors examine an early GM Wankel rotary engine, displayed in 1973.

tant criteria. Among the advantages of the rotary engine, Dr. Cole listed size, weight, simplicity, fewer components, simple induction system with better breathing, wider engine speed range, lower friction, better balance, and more favorable fuel and lubrication requirements.

Dr. Cole admitted that the fuel economy question was the most talked-about problem, saying, "You will find no more controversial subject or engineering problem than fuel economy." However, Dr. Cole told the conference that 80 percent of the fuel economy problem in the rotary engine has been traced to seal leakage. These problems, he promised, can be solved by the study and discovery of the right materials for the engine components.

"Ultimately," Dr. Cole added, "treated cast-iron for the housing is the goal of people working on the rotary engine."

As far back as the spring of 1972, officials of Mobil Oil Corporation, New York, reported to the annual meeting of the National Petroleum Refiners Association that in addition to Toyo Kogyo's large production of rotary engines (about 40,000 per month in 1974) the huge Comotor plant in Europe's Ruhr Valley was tooling up with a design capacity of 3,000 engines per day (about a million a year) and that Fiat of Italy had contracted for 300,000 of those engines per year. With the prospect of more than 500,000 U.S. engines coming off the assembly lines by 1975, Mobil's report concluded:

> We expect that the rotary will become one of the standard engines for automobiles and pleasure boats in the next few years, and that its lubrication and fuel problems will become a normal part of our thinking and planning.

In 1972, in GM's "Report on Progress in Areas of Public Concern," Robert J. Templin, then general project manager of GM's special product development group (the group then in charge of developing the company's rotary-combustion engine), cited packaging, weight, manufacturing flexibility, and operating characteristics as the main advantages of the rotary

130

engine. With a farsighted reference toward future pollution-control problems, Templin emphasized the engine's packaging qualities with these words:

> The engine is smaller and lighter than current automotive piston engines of comparable output. The dimensions of a 200 cu. in. rotary engine are about half those of the 140 cu. in. (piston) Vega L-4, the smallest GM engine in U.S. production. On the basis of output, this rotary engine is more comparable to our production 6-cylinder engine but weighs 30 percent less. Thus lighter, more compact vehicles can be designed around rotary engines. This will be a necessity in the '70's and '80's because of the addition of bulky pollution-control devices as well as the need for free crush space in the front of the vehicle to satisfy barrier-crash requirements.

In the July 1972 *Fortune*, Templin was quoted as saying that the rotary engine is "the only path we know to simultaneously improve fuel economy, vehicle performance, and emissions."

From another quarter came a report that was also complimentary to the Wankel, this time in *American Medical News*, published by the American Medical Association. In its March 20, 1972 issue the prestigious weekly newspaper said that the AMA's committee on the medical aspects of automotive safety believes that the Wankel engine has significant potential as far as health is concerned. Remarking that this was not an official stand, the committee's chairman, Dr. William K. Keller, said, "Eventually, we will be forced to switch to some fuel source other than petroleum. But until that time, a little engine has definite advantages over a larger one." In reference to pollution problems and the packaging situation, he continued:

> Manufacturers will be able to add a considerable amount of anti-pollution equipment to the little engine without increasing the weight or size of the automobile [beyond present-day specifications]. Thus [with the Wankel] engineers are far less limited in the extent to which they can go in the development of "cleaning" equipment.

131

### The Wankel Rotary Engine

Ford Motor Company, which has alternately negotiated for Wankel licenses and told the press it would have nothing to do with the Wankel, presented a report of its own activities to the U.S. Environmental Protection Agency on March 5, 1973 that covered the work the company said it was doing in the area of automotive pollution control. The report covered Ford's work—on which the company said it had spent $55 million in the past five years and planned to spend an additional $24.5 million, a 20 percent increase over the preceding year, in 1973—in investigating ten different kinds of alternatives to the present-day power sources. One of the alternatives—number eight on the list—was the Wankel engine. Ford said that it had been testing Mazda engines in attempts to develop emissions systems. The report spoke of such problems as increasing gas-fuel ratios in order to meet NOx standards only to find that the resulting exhaust temperatures were too low to support sufficient unburned-hydrocarbon and carbon monoxide oxidation; and further, that unacceptable driveability was encountered. The company said it had two vehicles with rotary engines (Mazda RX-2's) that were behind schedule in testing because of engine failures caused by ingestion of insulation materials that had been recirculated to the engine through an experimental system Ford had applied to it. Ford concluded, in its report to the government, that "once feasibility is established 36 months will be required to incorporate the Wankel approach in production."

Switching for a moment from automobiles, more than passing attention is due Outboard Marine Corporation, which already has thousands of rotary-powered snowmobiles in the hands of customers, and which hopes to offer various sizes of outboard motor-boat engines sometime after 1974. S. L. Metcalf, director of marine engineering for OMC, has spoken frequently of the low-cost potential of the rotary engine, but he says it cannot be realized until machine tools are developed and standardized manufacturing processes are refined. OMC, he said in 1973, will not introduce rotary engines in its other lines unless economic as well as technical considerations can be met.

Referring to an upcoming marine unit now under serious consideration, he said, "Achieving the full cost potential of the RC engine is vital, for we do not believe the average customer will pay a premium for novelty alone." With past records of millions of sales to pleasure-boat customers, he added, "After all, an engine is an engine, and as long as it pushes a boat or snowmobile quietly, reliably, and economically, the average owner doesn't care whether its pistons go up and down or around and around." He continued:

> The rotary must give us both manufacturing and sales advantages in a large market on any product for which it is designed. Where the RC engine can be designed and developed to give decided advantages in performance and cost, it will be applied to our other products. The rotary-combustion engine being developed today in our engineering laboratories must meet—and exceed—the competition of our present light and compact 2-cycle engines, or there will be no justification for a change.

On this cautious note, having already become the first American manufacturer to market Wankel engines—on snowmobiles—OMC is proceeding with its RC marine engine program, beginning with racing. There is no question in the author's mind but that OMC rotary motor-boat engines are just over the horizon.

At the same presentation with Metcalf, Charles D. Strang, group vice president, marine products, of OMC, had this to say about his company's marine activities:

> The mere process of bringing this engine to a stage where it is fit to start competing has already advanced our RC development program far beyond its original schedule—all of which is aimed specifically at bringing the RC outboard to the boating consumer at the earliest possible time consistent with a quality product of proven durability.

133

### The Wankel Rotary Engine

A couple of years ago the Oldsmobile general manager, John Beltz, disclosed to a group of Detroit newsmen that he visualized the time when a compact Olds would be powered by a Wankel engine. He put it this way: "I think the Wankel, in the present state of development, belongs in a small car, and is not suited for any cars we are building now at Oldsmobile." And now that Oldsmobile has a small car ready for it, one might ask, can the rotary-Olds be far off?

Widely-read *Automotive News*, the "bible" among people in the auto industry, prints something about the Wankel every week, and most issues contain several stories relating to the rotary's present state and future possibilities. In an editorial in mid-1972 the prominent news-weekly cited the advantages of the Wankel to the stylists because of its small size and made a strong point regarding its manufacturing economies. But the main thrust of the editorial dealt with world-wide logistics and why they were important to General Motors, the world's largest manufacturer. The overwhelming advantage of fewer parts—which means less tooling, a smaller number of components to automate for assembly or to route, handle, and ship around the world—was pointed out. Reduced stocking problems and fewer servicing problems were mentioned. And finally, the fact of the Wankel's lower octane requirement— spread over a world-wide situation—was considered valuable in solving future fuel logistics problems because, as the editorial pointed out, "The Wankel can run on local stuff, no matter where."

At the 1973 Chevrolet press introduction, John Z. DeLorean, recently promoted to a vice-presidency at General Motors, admitted that Chevrolet officials felt the Wankel engine was "a strong contender for the future," but he was not ready to predict what share of the market the rotary powerplant will command by 1980. He was asked whether the engine, scheduled to be an option on the 1975 Chevrolet Vega, would be sold in large numbers during the first year of production. "General Motors does not experiment with the public," he replied. "We are very enthusiastic about the Wankel. I think that if they were available now, we could sell any number of them in the Vegas. That's because it's a wonderful, smooth engine."

DeLorean said that he expected that GM would soon have "hundreds" of Wankel engines running "in various configurations" for testing purposes, mentioning that "approximately twenty" were then already in action. Asked about the market for 1980, he quickly replied that an answer would be "rank speculation," adding that the Wankel could "wind up to be 60 percent of our business—or 10 percent." It was almost at that moment that the first RC engines, for snowmobiles, began coming off the assembly lines of Evinrude Motors Division of OMC in Milwaukee—the first Wankels to be engineered and mass-produced in the United States.

Every sentence in the press containing the word "Wankel" seemed to provoke reams of new speculation about the future of the new engine. There were apparently three camps—those who for obscure corporate purposes were talking it down, those who for public-relations purposes were leaking small and cautious notes of optimism to the hungry press, and a few individuals of integrity who were making bold statements regarding the ultimate "takeover" of the Wankel. Among the last group is Robert Brooks.

Brooks is a management consultant with John Gustafson and Company of Chicago. He flatly predicted a complete change-over to the Wankel in this nation by the year 1980. Busy in 1972 and 1973 conducting seminars on the Wankel for interested corporations and securities analysts, Brooks said that a typical Wankel produced in the United States would cost about $100 less to produce than a piston engine of comparable size.

"After development costs are paid for, the savings will help defray part of the high cost of government-required safety and emissions equipment," he said. The small size and light weight of the Wankel," he continued, "will greatly simplify the change to a new type of car with engine, transmission, and driveline components in the front, driving the front wheels. Such cars

**135**

will have better traction and better steering, and they will provide more passenger space."

Brooks pointed to the somewhat easier task of controlling emissions from the Wankel, and he made quite a point of the Wankel's ability to run on very low-octane unleaded gasoline. "The changeover to Wankel-type engines," he said, "will possibly come soon enough to save the oil industry from having to spend hundreds of millions of dollars for new refinery equipment otherwise needed to produce the higher-priced, unleaded, higher-octane gasoline required by conventional engines that will be fitted soon with catalytic converters."

Adding that the low-octane gasoline for the Wankel will cost less to make and could be sold for slightly less than the price of current regular grades, Brooks said, "This advantage to the consumer and the oil industry will be lost, however, if the timetable established in current exhaust-emission legislation is not altered to recognize the new factor that the Wankel will be in almost all cars produced after the very tight 1975–76 emissions specifications go into effect."

In 1972 Brooks said that both General Motors and Ford were working at top speed to refine the Wankel, then tool up to produce it. The three largest auto makers in Japan, as well as many European manufacturers, he stated, were working toward the same target.

Asked why, after fifteen years of development effort, the future of the Wankel suddenly seemed, to him, so good, Brooks replied: "Recent breakthroughs in materials and manufacturing methods have now made possible the production of truly low-cost Wankels that have excellent reliability and long service life. Some of these materials are so good, in fact, that development of diesel versions (on which Felix Wankel is currently reported to be working) will soon get under way in earnest."

As this book goes to press, more speculation on General Motors and its potentially enormous role in the future of Felix Wankel's invention has occurred. Now the predictions go

**136**

beyond the Vega car and center on GM's coming out with a rotary-equipped Camaro sporty car for the 1975 model year. The latest rumors speak of a two-rotor engine of 3,380 cubic centimeters having a horsepower output at the shaft of 140 at 6,300 rpm. None of this speculation is confirmed by General Motors, but it is from good sources and likely to be accurate. Remember that all official words from GM have spoken of the Vega as the first car likely to be offered with a rotary engine. But General Motors must respond to Ford's slimmed-down Mustang II in the same way it responded (somewhat belatedly) to the original Mustang with its Camaro. The new, smaller Camaro projected to be marketed in the fall of 1974 as a 1975 model is also an excellent candidate for the RC engine when GM finally decides to offer it to the public.

Keeping in mind the all-powerful marketing potential of General Motors, however, it is not unreasonable to assume that the corporation will do more than one thing with the Wankel in 1974. And it would be logical to market the GM RC as an option in the Vega and, if production showed signs of being able to handle the load, as a standard engine in the Camaro, a good-looking little car sporty enough to deserve the mounting of an engine that is bound to make automotive history.

Only time—and a massive public relations campaign—will tell. But this you can bet on: General Motors won't fool around. That corporation will come out with a rotary package that will sell, a package that will be distributed throughout the corporate setup. Ford and Chrysler—and eventually American Motors—will have to follow as soon as they can.

Meantime, with a five-year lead, Mazda expects to benefit from the "new" upsurge in interest in the rotary engine. So far, Mazda has done everything right, and it's a safe expectation that Toyo Kogyo's pattern of providing innovative and dependable transportation to the American public will continue uninterrupted. Toyo Kogyo's Director Shigemi puts it this way: "We are anticipating the next few years with much pleasure."

# Bibliography

BOOKS

Ansdale, Richard F.: *The Wankel RC Engine*. A. S. Barnes & Co., South Brunswick & New York, first American edition, 1969.

Automobile Manufacturers Assn. Inc. (now Motor Vehicle Manufacturers Assn. of the U.S.): *Automobiles of America*. Wayne State University Press, Detroit, 1962.

Donovan, Frank: *Wheels for a Nation*. Thomas Y. Crowell Co., New York, 1965.

Glenn, Harold T.: *Exploring Power Mechanics*. Chas. A. Bennett Co., Inc., Peoria, 1962.

*History of Research and Development on Mazda Rotary Engine*. Toyo Kogyo Co. Ltd., Hiroshima, 1972.

Jamison, Andrew: *The Steam-Powered Automobile, An Answer to Air Pollution*. Indiana University Press, Bloomington & London, 1971.

## The Wankel Rotary Engine

L'Editrice Dell'Automobile LEA, Editor: *World Cars*. The Automobile Club of Italy & Herald Books, Bronxville, 1972.

Matteucci, Marco: *History of the Motor Car*. Crown Publishers, Inc., New York & Turin, 1970.

Norbye, Jan P.: *The Wankel Engine, Design, Development, Applications*. Chilton Book Co., Philadelphia, New York, London, 1971.

*Rotary Engines*. Toyo Kogyo Co. Ltd., Hiroshima, 1971.

Stein, Ralph: *The Treasury of the Automobile*. Golden Press, New York, 1961.

Stern, Philip Van Doren: *A Pictorial History of the Automobile*. The Viking Press, New York, 1953.

ARTICLES

"Brief Test: Mazda RX-2 Automatic." *Road & Track*, February, 1973.

Burck, Charles G.: "A Car That May Reshape the Industry's Future." *Fortune*, July, 1972.

Dunne, Jim: "GM Rotary Engine for the '74 Vega." *Popular Science*, May, 1972.

Ethridge, John: "50,000-Mile Mazda R-100 Rotary Tear-Down Report." *Road Test*, January, 1972.

"Introducing: GM's 1975 Rotary Combustion Engine." *Road Test*, September, 1973.

"Is the Wankel the Auto Engine of the Future?" *Changing Times*, July, 1972.

Pond, James B.: "OMC's Men and Their RC Machine." *Automotive Industries*, May 15, 1972.

Roe, Jim: "First Report: PS Drives OMC's Hot New Stack-of-Wankels Outboard." *Popular Science*, June, 1973.

Smith, Dave: "Chrysler Tells WWR Why It's Lukewarm on Wankels." *Ward's Wankel Report*, August 25, 1972.

"Two Electrodes Cut Mazda Plug Wear." *Ward's Wankel Report*, July 28, 1972.

"Wangle Yourself a Wankel." *Forbes*, December 15, 1972.

"What's a Wankel?" *Ward's Wankel Report*, July 13, 1973.

# Index

# Index

exhaust emission control system, Mazda, 120
exhaust products, 10, 25

Fiat (company), 24, 130
Fifth National Automobile Show, 15
financing, automobile, 16
Ford (automobile), 15
Ford (company), 24, 26, 53, 79, 80, 81, 132, 137
Ford (company) Wankel development, 136
Ford engineers, 7
Ford, Henry, 6, 7, 17
Ford, Henry II, 80, 81
Ford-Werke AG (company), 81
fossil-fuel (energy), 21
four-cycle engine, 14
Franklin (automobile), 15
Froede, Dr. Walter, 58, 82
fuel economy problems, general, 130
fuel, liquid, 14

"gas buggy," 3
gasoline, direct service, 15
gasoline retailers: closings down, 42; "strike," 42; "shutdowns," 42
gasoline shortage, 41
gas turbine, 10, 24; aircraft, 89; disadvantages in autos, 24; marine, 71
gas wars, 41
General Motors, 16, 24, 26, 46, 50, 77, 83; future Wankel development, 136; RC license, 83–84; RC project, 51, 84–87; world-wide logistics, 134
General Motors RC engine: general description, 131; other advantages, 86; pollution control, 86; power-to-bulk ratio, 84; power-to-weight ratio, 86
General Motors Research Corporation, 17
General Motors Technical Center, 84
*Genussscheine*, 82
Goering, Hermann, 57
Great Depression, 5
Gremlin (automobile), 76
Gustafson, John, and Co., 135

Haagen-Smit, Dr. A. J., 33
Haas, Dr. Wilhelm, 63
heat engines, 9

Hitler, Adolf, 57
Hollier (automobile), 16
horsepower race, 18
Hudson, 6
Hutzenlaub, Ernest, 82
hydrocarbon (energy), 21
hydrocarbons, unburned, 18, 25, 91
hydroelectric dams, 4
hydroelectric (energy), 21

ignition timing, rotary engine, 123
Imperial (automobile), 38
Indianapolis 500, 11
installment paper, 16

Jackson (automobile), 16
Japan Automatic Transmission Company, 79
jet engines (aircraft), 24, 89
Johnson (rotary engine), 71, 74
Junkers (company), 57

Kauertz, Eugene (German) engine, 49
Keller, Dr. Wm. K., 131
Kettering, Charles, 17
King (automobile), 16
KKM (engine), 58, 60
KKM prototype, 58–62; roughness, 65; smoke, 65; "chatter marks," 65

Langen, Eugene, 13
Langen-Otto (automobile), 14
Lenoir, Etienne, 3
Leyland (of England), 24
liquid fuel, 14
Locomobile, 15
Lonrho, Ltd., 82
Loofbourrow, Alan G., 77
Los Angeles Basin, 32, 33
Luftwaffe, 57
lugging, engine, 109

manual shifting, automobile, 108
Marcus, Siegfried, 3
marine RC engine, 72, 74
mass production (gasoline automobiles), 14
Matsuda, Kohei, 81
Matsuda, Tsuneji, 64
Maverick (automobile), 81

SUMMER 77

INVENTORY 1983